YOU'RE ON NEXT!

YOU'RE ON NEXT!

How to survive on television and radio

Michael Bland

**Kogan
Page**

To Penny

First published 1979
by Kogan Page Ltd
120 Pentonville Road, London N1

Distributed in the United States of America by
Nichols Publishing Company
Post Office Box 96, New York, NY 10024

Copyright © 1979 Michael Bland

Printed in Great Britain by
The Anchor Press Ltd, Tiptree, Essex

ISBN 0 85038 164 9

Acknowledgements

I am immensely grateful to the people who have helped with this book. Particular thanks are due to: Michael Blakstad (BBC) for contributing, George Bull (*Director* magazine) for permission to publish Michael Blakstad's article, Tomas Cernikowsky (Reuters) for the idea of the book, Dorothy Drake (Confederation of British Industry) for contributing, Johna Pepper (Ford Motor Company) for a load of information, John Swinfield (Anglia Television) for contributing, Huw Thomas (Huw Thomas and Associates) for expert advice, and Penny and Win, my chief typists.

Contents

1. Big brother is looking for you

It's all-powerful. Reputations are lost in seconds on it. Powerful people turn to jelly at the thought of it. Tough businessmen will run miles to hide from it.

It's television. The phenomenon which has changed our lives in the last 40 years is still finding its place in society. Some see it as a blessing to education and understanding, while others blame it for the divorce rate, violence and bad eyesight.

All the controversy, though, concerns the people who *watch* television and the people who *make* the programmes. While they haggle over the quality of the material, audience ratings, networks and advertising, no one thinks about the person in the middle — the respectable citizen who for one reason or another suddenly finds himself in a studio providing the entertainment for everyone else.

And that person could be you. Television's appetite for victims is insatiable and the likelihood is increasing for everyone that at some time in their lives they will be interviewed on the box.

The number of television stations is growing all the time. Almost every country in the world has at least one network, while the developed countries have not only national networks but an ever-increasing array of regional ones.

The US is a big place, but it's still staggering to realize that it has no less than a thousand television stations. Even in already over-saturated regions the viewer will cheerfully accept as many channels as can be built into the set.

In Britain a fourth national channel is imminent despite the old films and replays with which the existing channels are padded, and some active communities which are too far from their 'local' station for it to be local are demanding a channel of their own.

There is more variety in the programmes, too. Science, economics, money, business are relative newcomers, and we are in the early days of companies and groups of people making their own programmes.

There are more TV sets and more viewers. What was an exciting novelty for the privileged few only a generation ago is now an indispensable part of most people's lives. The mind boggles at the influence it will have a generation from now.

People have more watching time. The four-day week is becoming a reality, there are more televisions in schools and there are even TVs in some factories. The set which used to bring you flickering old Errol Flynn films can now be adapted to retrieve the horse-racing results, news flashes, weather forecasts or stock market prices at the touch of a button.

Some stations already have the 'mini-cam' — a complete live outside broadcast unit operated by one person. RCA predict that by the early 1980s mini-cams will be on the market for all and sundry at about $30 apiece.

With the growth of television the demand is growing for people to appear on it, along with an increasing small band of volunteers who are one step ahead of the game and getting to TV before it gets to them.

It adds up to one message: every day it becomes a little more likely that *you* will find yourself in front of the cameras.

This is especially true for businessmen. They are still a tiny group of television performers compared with the heavies like politicians and trade unionists, but television and business are just waking up to each other's existence. The percentage growth of businessmen appearing on television is possibly higher than for any other group.

Growing it may be, but people are still terrified of it for a number of reasons.

First, there are the horror stories. We've all seen them: an inexperienced spokesman dies the death of a thousand cuts in front of 20 million people. Someone campaigning for a good cause is made to look a fanatic by skilful editing. A devoted public servant comes over as a bumbling idiot thanks to some loaded questions. And a businessman who has put his prices up to stay alive is turned into a grasping capitalist by a vicious interviewer.

Most of us are uneasy about the alien environment, too. Television studios are so unfamiliar: the lights, the cameras, the trendy people, the clutter, the hassle. Walking into a studio the average first-timer feels like a pink-fleshed missionary entering an Amazon head-hunting village.

Nor do we like being made fools of. For verbal bad eggs and visual rotten tomatoes, television is the hottest thing since the village stocks.

And lastly there's that stomach-vibrating fear of a large audience. Anyone who has been in a school play or had to make a speech knows how he goes all to pieces when hundreds of eyes are fixed on him.

Therefore, most unprepared people going on television are doomed to be below their best. But you're going to be caught by it some day, so why not meet it head-on now?

It's a discipline of its own. There's a lot to learn, and a few tips from George who 'went on' a couple of years ago just aren't enough.

You too can beat them at their own game.

2. What's so different about television?

At first sight it's perfect. Television brings the outside world with all its colour and sound right into your home.

If you sit in a studio, a camera and microphone receive your image and voice and convert them into an electronic signal. This signal is then transmitted to your TV set and converted back into its original form. Everything is faithfully conveyed — face, colour, dress, mannerisms, voice, tone, the lot.

But out of all the thousands of characteristics that are brought so instantly and accurately to the living room the most important is lost somewhere in the air between the camera and the set: personality.

Think about it next time you watch a top businessman on television. Would he frighten you? Hell no, yet to have got where he has that guy must have some kind of hold over people, some extra drive that simply doesn't come through on the airwaves.

How often do you hear people say: 'He comes over much better face to face'? Quite often, too, the converse is true, and apparently lively entertainers seem disappointingly ordinary when you meet them in the flesh.

Either way, television deprives you of your real personality and gives you a completely different one.

It does funny things with your normal, often subconscious, ways of communicating. A quizzical raising of the eyebrows can make you look as if you're clowning around. A reflective pause comes over as an evasive search for a sneaky answer. The 'ums' and 'ers' which we use all the time in normal conversation become an infuriating distraction. Unobtrusive shadows under the eyes are converted into cadaverous hollows.

So those who succeed at appearing on television fall into two categories:
1. those whose image as it appears on the set is accidentally pleasing to the viewer, and
2. those who work at getting their image right.

If you are one of the chosen few in the first category a great career awaits you. But if you belong, with the rest of us, in the second category, keep reading.

The audience is different, too. Mostly you have to communicate with the viewer after work when he is relaxing at home. There are plenty of distractions and the box in the corner of the room is expected to entertain. In a face-to-face conversation you have some hold over the other person, but when you're on television the viewer can be as rude as he likes. He can simply press a button and make you disappear.

Just to complicate things further, television journalists are a different breed. Very basically, their task is similar to their newspaper counterparts. Their job is to report happenings, to describe things and to comment. The reporting must be correct, the descriptions accurate and interesting and the comment informed.

However, television imposes some extra rules on these journalists. The viewer is not satisfied with second-hand descriptions but wants to see things for himself. The deadlines are more immediate and more frequent than those of a newspaper.

The biggest difference is with interviewing. A newspaper journalist can discuss things at length with you and distil the results into a short piece. The television interviewer not only has to interview you; he also has to make the interview entertaining. This means a lot more cut-and-thrust. As we shall see later, a tough interview is advantageous, but the unaccustomed interviewee takes it as a personal affront.

Because it's different, television needs a whole new approach and the purpose of this book is to demonstrate some techniques for improving your performance, handling interviews and communicating with the viewer.

It's about how to *exploit* television instead of being terrified and humiliated by it.

It may seem strange that radio has been left till the end of the book despite its considerable importance and the similar techniques. But it's simpler to learn about television first, embracing all the main techniques, and then look at radio and its differences. That way we don't keep switching from one to the other.

So don't switch off as soon as you've finished the television stuff. Radio has plenty of advantages of its own and should be treated with equal respect and enthusiasm.

Now, back to television.

3. Why use television?

Television is like a tiger — great to look at but terrifying to get involved with.

Thousands of businessmen and leaders of pressure groups, chambers of commerce, fund-raisers and political associations go through life assuming that 'TV is for the pros', that they themselves are doing well if they make half a column in the local paper.

Well, all that is changing. With more and more stations on more and more channels putting out more and more programmes, there is room on the screen for almost anybody with something interesting to say.

Many people will have bought this book as a defensive gesture, looking for guidance on how to survive when they are dragged kicking and screaming into the studios. You won't be disappointed if that's all you want, but there's so much more you can achieve with television.

So far, television simply uses us. Yet like all things it is there to be used *by* us. It is nothing more than a communications medium which is always searching for entertaining material. Almost anybody can use it to get a message into millions of homes — free.

For the businessman it can be a public relations tool or it can be the death of the business, depending on how it is treated. The same company director who uses other publicity media with the skill of the born salesman will retreat in terror from a heaven-sent opportunity to display his firm or product to a vast clientele through a highly credible medium.

Certainly television is 'different', but it is also a challenging and important medium through which a small but increasing number of companies are learning to promote their goods, to scotch rumours and to reassure people. It can also be used (a major advertising plus) to instil the company's name in people's subconscious minds.

Let's not get completely carried away. There's going to be the odd occasion when you want to keep a low profile and will have good cause to steer clear of the screen. But the vast majority of times when businessmen refuse to go on television, it is on a pretext which boils down to: 'They'll ask a lot of awkward questions and make me look a fool.'

And that's the heart of it: 'I might be made to look a fool.' It's understandable, but hardly enterprising.

Successful business is all about seizing opportunities. Television is a glorious opportunity to promote business. The time has come to be businesslike about it, to learn the ground rules, get to know the people who make the programmes, work out how to relate the medium to your business, and have a determined go at it.

It's the same story whether the news is good or bad. If it's bad — if they are probing into a strike, a fire, a duff product, excess profits — there's no excuse for absence. One of the few certainties is that your absence is something that will damn you.

By having a go you stand at least a chance of putting some or all of the record straight, and of diverting the viewer's attention to another, more positive, aspect of the business. If you take cover you are asking for the Star Chamber by innuendo. Without you there to answer back, the presenters, interviewers, union leaders and 'experts' will have a field day.

Incredibly, businessmen run away even when it's good news. Often a programme which genuinely wants to show a company and its goods in a favourable light has the door slammed in its face by reluctant management who 'don't want a lot of cameras all over the place'.

Businessmen aren't the only ones for whom television presents a golden opportunity. For example, anyone running a pressure group who has not put that group's case over on TV should go in for a little self-examination. Whether you believe in equality for a minority, free housing, capital punishment, a flat earth or more sexual freedom for the Greater Horseshoe Bat, you should be in there getting your message over.

It's a game almost anyone can play. Trade associations can

show their importance, politicians glean votes, scientists air their knowledge, churchmen win souls, planners get public understanding and government officials bore us to death.

Dr Goebbels would have given his saluting arm for a television in every home, yet now they're there for all to use.

4. Preparation and briefing

To go or not to go

It's happened. You have just had lunch and are getting stuck into the afternoon's work. At first you think the voice on the phone is a friend pulling a practical joke: 'Hello, my name is Ruth Less. I'm a researcher for the 'Look Round' programme. We've heard about the new factory you're building and I wonder if you could do an interview?'

Other than shouting 'Help!', what's the first thing to do? Well, for a start:

Ring back
This girl is trying to push you into an instant decision. Would you say yes or no on the spot if it was a business transaction? It is best to get the basic details and have a quick think, so be businesslike — ask Ms Less some questions:

☐ What time do you want me for?
☐ Where?
☐ How long will it take?
☐ Who will be doing the interview?

Write down the answers. Now, unless you are quite certain, tell her: 'It looks possible, but I'll have to call you back. Give me just five minutes. Can I have your phone number?'

This has given you a few minutes of vital breathing space. Use it, but don't go mad . . . many a person has lost the big opportunity by saying yes too late. Devote those ten minutes of breathing space to making a quick decision on what you are going to tell Ms Less.

Rationalize it
1. *Are you available or aren't you?* If not, could you *make*

yourself available? If you can't do it tonight, is there another time that you could? Or could you go in and record the programme some other time today when you *are* available? If you really can't make it, is there someone else you could send?

If the answer in all cases is no, then you have no choice but to apologize — *and tell them honestly why you can't make it.* Be sure that they know you want to help and that they can try you again.

But if you are going to take this TV business seriously, then a lot of things which would normally be good reasons for not going are simply no excuse for turning down a chance to put your case over to a few million people.

Dinner parties, golf games, nagging wives, demanding mistresses, headaches and the week's shopping may be pressing, but they must take second place. Worse still, if you're successful enough at business to be wanted by the TV people then you're probably permanently busy, and it might mean cancelling an important engagement.

It is more likely that, by fair means or foul, you can make it. If so, what next?

2. *Do you want to do it?* Put it on the scales:

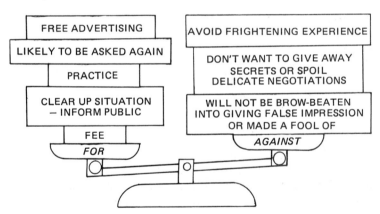

The scales *should* tip in favour. If they don't, *give them a bit of a nudge* — if only for one reason: the most chilling sound, one of the most damning things that can happen to you, the undoing of years of hard work, is the sentence: 'A spokesman for the company would not comment.' When you hear those fearful words after refusing to talk, you will wish that you had put your fingers on the scales when making that decision.

'So', you ask, 'if I've already decided to accept, what was the point of weighing the pros and cons in the first place?' There are two reasons:

(a) If you first convince yourself that it is right to accept, then everything that follows can be tackled with much more enthusiasm because you know *why* you are doing it.
(b) There just *might* be a genuine reason for saying no. It is unlikely, but it is better to have checked than to find out half-way through the interview.

Tell them of your decision

While you have been weighing the pros and cons, Ruth Less has been thumbing through her contacts cards for alternative interviewees, so get back to her right away. Tell her that you will do it — and now it is time to get something in return for the favour. It is essential to be firm with these people because they are in a business where liberties are bound to be taken. People who are approached by TV programmes tend to fall into two categories:

(a) those who are aloof and intransigent — so the TV people end up saying 'to hell with you, we'll get someone else', or
(b) those who let themselves be pushed around and would stand on their heads and bark so long as it pleased these new gods of the silver screen.

The secret is to aim between the two extremes. Most TV types are reasonable, down-to-earth journalists — only a very few are looking for trouble — but until you know the individuals better and can relax a bit (or get tougher), treat them all in the same way — like business acquaintances. It pays to be friendly but to guard your speech. It *never* pays to try to outsmart them.

Ask them
You have a right to be a little demanding — after all, you are effectively going into a business contract with them.

You already know where and for how long, but make Ms Less pay for your trouble by telling you:

☐ *Why* are they doing this programme?

☐ Why *me*?

☐ What is their source of information? If it's a press cutting, ask them to read it to you so that they don't confront you later with an unexpected piece of information.

☐ Is it to be live or recorded?

☐ Will they be using any film or props that you should know about?

☐ *Who else* is going on the programme (such as a competitor or customer)?

☐ Can they give you an idea of the questions?

They won't give you a list of the questions word for word, of course. The exact form of the questions is usually only decided at the last minute, and if the interviewer finds an interesting line of discussion during the programme, it is his job to probe further and forget the original questions. Besides, if you know the exact questions in advance you're heading for one almighty boring interview.

There was an example on British television some years ago where the interviewer was facing a famous and ponderous architect. He wrote out his five questions on five cards and gave copies to his subject to prepare answers. At the last second the producer cut the interview from five minutes to three. It made sense to the interviewer to head straight into questions three, four and five. To his horror the architect mechanically intoned his prepared answers to questions one, two and three. If nothing else, the interview had a touch of originality to it!

However, they *should* have an idea of the *sort* of questions they want to ask. Television interviewers are professionals. So are their research teams, and they will already be thinking about their line of questioning. This at least will give you an idea. If they say (and they often will): 'Oh, we haven't really worked out our questions yet' (probably true at that moment), then say you'll ring back in half an hour to get an idea. There's no law to say they have to give you an idea of the questions, but there is some moral obligation to do so.

Once you have the line of questioning, don't treat it as gospel for they may well deviate, usually for genuine reasons. But at least you now have a guide.

Shock Horror

'Thanks a lot', says Ms Less, 'we'll see you at 6.00 tonight. Goodbye.'

Click.

The feeling is not unlike watching the judge donning his black cap.

Consolation: it grabs everyone like that. If you don't feel nervous or at least apprehensive about doing the programme, then ask yourself very seriously if you're the right person to be doing it. The biggest clangers are dropped by the people who think they know it all. Even experienced campaigners should get that slightly sick feeling. It is best counteracted by filling in the time with thorough preparation. Now:

Prepare, prepare, prepare . . .

And again prepare. There is no such thing as over-preparation.

Never, but never, attempt to 'play it by ear'. You will be crucified if you do. In some ways it is disadvantageous to do a programme on your own specialist subject, because it is one thing to know an enormous amount about a subject and quite another to have your mind ordered and equipped to present that knowledge.

Try it and see. Take your favourite subject, buttonhole a friend and impart your knowledge of it, without preparation, in two minutes, in the most effective way you can. Now do it again with another friend, having first planned what you are going to say on the basis of this chapter. Then test your friends to see which one grasped the most!

Ideally you should allow at least an hour for preparation. Even if they want you at once, you *must* take a few minutes to get it all clear in your head. Get a taxi round the block, hide in the lavatory, anything, but never rush straight into the studio, like a sacrificial virgin, with a blank mind and a hitherto unblemished record.

As the seconds tick past it becomes increasingly difficult to put your thoughts in order. Dr Johnson said that a hanging concentrates the mind wonderfully. In many respects a television interview may *seem* like a public hanging, but it certainly doesn't concentrate the mind. The temptation is to do anything *but* concentrate on a thorough, well-rehearsed brief.

Think

Now, with time to get ready for this thing, sit down, shut the door, take the phone off the hook, and *think*. The first thing to get into your head is: *you are not going there to defend yourself.*

No matter how friendly the programme, be it face-to-face, phone-in, panel, down-the-line, film or whatever, at some stage you will find yourself feeling you have to justify your existence.

☐ 'Surely, Mrs Smith, this is all a bit unnecessary, isn't it?. . .'
☐ 'Mr Jones, it could be argued that . . .'
☐ 'We, the public, would like to know why you . . .'
☐ 'This is all very well, Mr Doe, but . . .'

and so on. The friendliest interviewer has at least one devil's advocate question on his notepad. But, as you will see later, this is not a court of law or a friendly pub you are going to. It is a communication medium with rules of its own. So start saying it now: *I am going there to say what I want to say, not what they want me to say,* and keep saying it.

Say what you want to say

The most important thing is to plan what it is you want to put over to all those people — because you are being given a golden opportunity to do so.

Tell the good news

Let us look at a couple of practical examples:

A businessman building a factory causes all sorts of problems — pollution, unsightly buildings, noise and the like. A programme about that factory is bound to mention these problems, but the man being interviewed has a different story to tell. He's providing jobs, he's paying rates and taxes, making an exciting new product — all beneficial stuff. It does not take much imagination to see that he and his company could benefit from going on the programme.

Or take a pressure group — say the director of a campaign for female equality. Is she going there to defend herself against accusations of being a bra-burning pain in the neck? Or is she going to use those three minutes to tell a couple of million other women that they are being treated like dirt and must make a stand against male piggery?

The most elementary grounding in public relations tells us

how to concentrate on the good news and avoid the bad. But the minute they feel the heat of the studio lights on their cheeks and hear the interviewer's distant voice, a lot of people forget this elementary principle and start to try to justify themselves.

It's so easy to forget, too, that although *you* know the good points of your company or organization, the other 3,999,999,999 on this earth do not.

Plan the message

Having thought what it is you want to say, it's time to think about *how* to communicate it. Write down your basic argument. Look, for example, at a vegetarian group. For years an exponent of vegetarianism has studied and expounded on the advantages of a vegetarian diet. His knowledge of the subject is vast. There is a wealth of things that the simple carnivore should be taught — economical vegetarian diets, suffering of animals, cholesterol damage, flavour and thousands of other things.

But now the requirement is to condense all this knowledge into a basic message. *At best you will get three points over.* So the philosophy is distilled into, for example:

1. Vegetables are better and cheaper than meat.
2. Animal food is bad for you.
3. There are not enough animals to go round.

These points are now to be the basis of everything you say during that interview. Whatever the questions, whatever the angle, you want to get these points over to the viewer. At this stage subsections can be added, for example:

1. Vegetables are better and cheaper.
   (a) Vegetables are half the cost of meat.
   (b) Vegetables contain all the protein and nutrients you need.
   (c) Vegetables are healthier because they contain roughage.
   (d) You can grow them in your own garden.

2. Animal foods are bad for you.
   (a) They contain large amounts of cholesterol.
   (b) etc.

By the time you have finished there should be three main points, each supported by three or four subpoints. If you know your subject you should be able to use that skeleton to get the main points of your message over in a couple of minutes — or to hold out for hours if you have to.

The important thing is: *each of those three main points must be able to stand up on its own,* because you might only have a few seconds in which to get it over.

Three is the optimum number. It can quite happily be only one or two, but go for the lower numbers rather than the higher ones. If you have four or five points to get over you will need (a) a lot of time, (b) a tolerant interviewer and (c) an abnormally receptive audience. The chances of getting it all together are more than remote.

We will look at *how* you get your points over in the chapter on 'Winning the battle'.

Distil the message

In all that you work for and believe in there must be a basic message. You start with a whole philosophy and distil it. It can then be distilled again and again until there is just one drop of 200-proof liquor. Look at the years of thinking and millions of words and figures that have gone into brief phrases like: 'What's good for General Motors is good for America'; '$E=MC^2$'; 'There is no such thing as a free lunch'; 'From each according to his ability, to each according to his needs.'

In *Animal Farm,* the pigs cut their whole initial philosophy down to 'four legs good, two legs bad' and made the sheep repeat it till they got it right. This is the principle to keep in mind when communicating something in a short space of time.

Limited time

It is human nature to try to communicate everything at once. Television, however, is like the stroboscopic lights on a rock group — a brief flash and you're gone. Next time you see an interview on television, watch for the amount of time the interviewee is given before the next question comes slamming in. What it boils down to is that you will have an average of about two minutes to say the *lot.*

Audience receptiveness

As well as having limited time at your disposal, you also have to contend with the state of mind of the people with whom you are trying to communicate. They are probably ironing, eating, reading, arguing, putting the kids to bed, thinking of changing channels. Even when the box has their undivided attention they are mentally relaxed and only concentrating at half volume.

This means you have to keep it *very* simple. It is not that they are stupid — simply that they are switched off. Clearly, some people watch some programmes on a high mental plane, but as a general guide research shows that the awareness of the average adult viewer while watching television is that of an alert teenager.

It is better to say the same thing several times than to say several things once.

Anecdotes

Here come the real weapons in your armoury. Which of the following statements has more impact?

☐ Animal fats are bad for you and can be fatal.
☐ A friend of mine died from eating animal fats.

The latter actually gives you a picture of some poor devil dying horribly from indulging in non-vegetarian activities.

Or, to get back to our business context, which of these do you think the viewers will relate to more?

☐ The new factory will improve local employment.
☐ Albert Jones bought his friends a drink today for the first time in three years; that's how long he was out of work before our factory was built.

The first one may be shorter, yet it has less impact than the second, because the latter makes you stop and listen.

This is because *people love stories.* Possibly the greatest communicator of all time was Christ. His philosophy is still grasped by hundreds of millions of people in all languages, 2000 years after his death — because he said it all in stories. For example, if he had just told people to have a care for those they did not like, the homily would have been forgotten by morning. So he told them about a Samaritan — a baddie — who took pity on a mugging victim. And the message still gets through today.

The examples are many. Look at the complex analysis of human relationships and attitudes contained in the short and simple story of the prodigal son.

So back to the brief. Point 1 was: Vegetables are better and cheaper, supported by: Vegetables are half the cost of meat.

You could now make this read: Vegetables are better and cheaper. Vegetables are half the cost of meat (wife . . . shopping). Because you are going to get that point over by saying: 'Do you know, last night I was on my own and felt like a treat, so I bought half a pound of steak, and it cost me a fortune. Now tonight my wife has got delicious baked potatoes topped with cheese and celery — for her *and* me *and* all four children, for *half* what that steak cost me.'

The point is that people *listen* to stories. They are also much more difficult for the interviewer to interrupt.

Ideally the story should be a true one, though it may be necessary to stretch things a bit to get the point over more forcibly. No one can challenge something like the wife and the vegetables, but beware of telling whoppers. It's easy to get carried away, and if you're caught out once, you've lost your credibility for the whole interview.

Analogies
Another effective way of communicating is to ring a bell in the other person's mind with something with which he is already familiar. Again, Christ was the master at this. How hard is it for a sinner to get into heaven? — as hard as it is for a camel to go through the eye of a needle. Or what better description of a false prophet than a 'ravening wolf dressed as a sheep'?

The most complex things can be reduced to simple ideas, and good analogies are ideal when time is short. Let's look at a few examples:

The editor of *The Times* was explaining (in his newspaper, actually, not on television) the highly complex theory of the relationship of the money supply to inflation over a period of time. Not easy, but hands up those who can't understand the following 35 words: 'The money supply is like a tap attached to a hosepipe which is two years long. Once the tap has been turned on at one end nothing can stop it coming out at the other.'

Or, using another example from the UK, take the spokesman for a pressure group to improve rail travel. He was deploring the fact that British Rail had bought a load of new engines at £80,000 each and then had no use for them. Instead of groping with meaningless figures he simply said: 'Do you realize that every one of those engines is a new primary school rusting in the sidings?' Immediate impact. No one feels very angry about a redundant railway engine, but when it is put in terms of children deprived of their education everyone gets emotional about it.

And that new factory we were talking about . . . what if for some reason you're building it in New Jersey. It's a very big factory. In fact, you tell the viewers, it's several hundred thousand square feet. That, to John Doe, who is reading the evening paper and shouting at the kids, means absolutely nothing. Tell him the factory is about the size of a baseball pitch and he can picture it at once.

The rules are simple. Look at every item in your brief and ask if it can be grasped immediately by a newcomer. Can it be improved? Can it be put into everyday terms? Does a reservoir contain 123,455,200 gallons of water or does it hold three weeks' supply for your town? Does the factory have an unpleasant aroma of sulphur dioxide or does it smell like bad eggs?

Learn the brief
So far so good. The first part of the preparation time has been spent thinking out why you are going on the programme, what it is you want to say and how to say it. There is always a temptation at this stage to say, 'Right, I've got that taped, now I'll go and have a drink.'

Hold it. We're only half way.

You know that terrible feeling when you have the answer to a question — it's on the tip of your tongue — but you cannot quite find the words or remember the details? Well, picture yourself in the same situation, sitting under the lights with the cameras relaying your embarrassment to the watching world.

This will not happen if you know your brief so well that a relevant passage springs to mind. We will soon be looking at how to get that particular message over regardless of the questions, but a fat lot of good it will do if you cannot remember what it was you wanted to say in the first place.

How long you spend boning up depends on how good your memory is, but you should not be satisfied until you know the brief by rote. By the time you go into the studio you should know your spiel, word for word.

Of course, there is going to be quite a bit of ad-libbing as you deal with the questions, but time and time again you will find yourself coming back to that prepared spiel, and being very glad of it.

Angle

News always seems to have an 'angle' — which is a position from which you only see part of the picture. Centuries of experience have taught journalists that people get bored with the whole picture, while a slant gives the story more interest. Many authorities are at work finding ways of presenting news and other programmes more fairly and in greater depth, but they have not found the answer yet. Hence this book.

The classic story about angle is the one about the Archbishop of Canterbury visiting New York. As he arrives at his hotel the reporters flock round and flood him with questions. One hack asks 'Your Grace, what do you think about the fact that there are rumoured to be call-girls in this hotel?' Horrified, the Archbishop asks '*Are* there any call-girls in my hotel?' Next day's headline: 'Archbishop's first question — "Are there any call-girls in my hotel?" '

It might seem a bit late at this stage to start worrying about their angle, but it has been left till now because *your* stuff is a whole lot more important than *theirs,* and also because you can never know for sure which way the interview will go. It's like an exam — if you try to prejudge the questions you might get it right and do well, but if you get them wrong you are in trouble.

So the best order of events is to be clear in your own mind what you want to say, then mentally to prepare some responses to certain potential questions.

There are two ways of getting an idea of the questions:

1. WHAT THEY SAID THEY WOULD ASK

This is why you asked Ms Less why they are doing this programme and what they were going to ask. Her reply might have been: 'We think it's an interesting story and will be asking you how much it's costing, what the local reaction is, what good it's going to do, your firm's accident record — you know, that sort of thing.' Up goes the red Verey flare. The angle here is that your factory is about to come under fire.

How much different would your answers be if she said: 'Oh, we want our viewers to know more about your operation. We'd like to know more about the product, how many jobs you'll provide, what sort of profit you expect from it, and such-like'?

It's simple — *your answers will be exactly the same.* That's what all the preparation was for, wasn't it?

But it helps to get an idea of the *trend* of their questions. Again, compare it to a business deal: when you go into a meeting to discuss a contract you like to know in advance what sort of reception you will get. The product you are selling is the same. The price you are asking is the same. But you will by instinct go out of your way to anticipate what the atmosphere at the meeting will be like and what sort of questions they are going to ask.

2. PUT YOURSELF IN THEIR SHOES

They have a job to do. Your job might be making money, or promoting a cause, or running the country. Theirs is to entertain and inform a lot of people. Consistently.

This thing you want to present on television — factory, theory, philosophy or whatever — pretend for a moment that you know nothing about it, yet you have the job of presenting it to the public by interviewing someone who does know something about it.

You will want to delve into what makes this person (ie, you) tick. Is it a good thing? a bad thing? Will it affect the way we live? What are the viewers going to think about it? Will it affect our health? our pockets? our sex lives?

Looked at this way some questions are virtually dead certs. Say the target is our friend the female liberationist:

☐ What do you hope to achieve by this movement?
☐ Are women really downtrodden? Do they need help?
☐ How many members does your organization have?
☐ What does your husband/lover think of this?

☐ What makes you think you are the right person for the job?

☐ What's your organization going to do — in practical terms — to achieve these aims?

Or that factory:

☐ What will it manufacture?

☐ Why are you building it? Why now?

☐ How big is it? What will it cost?

☐ Is it necessary?

☐ How long will it take to build?

☐ Is it going to make a lot of noise? smoke? smell?

☐ Will it have sports/social facilities?

So, a list of potential questions is a valuable guide and an important part of the preparation. Having thought some questions out, you again have to remember to *keep off that defensive hook.* Just as an appetizer for the next chapter, where we are going to learn how to use those questions to our advantage, take that sneaky question to the women's libber: 'What makes you think you are the right person for the job?' The temptation is to give a straight answer about why you think you are the best person to do it, thus the *defensive* answer might be: 'Well, I've spent my life campaigning for women's lib. I graduated in sociology, hate men, and have written two books on female equality . . .'

Now just where was all that nonsense in your prepared spiel? Nowhere, if you had any sense. The *positive* answer, in which you use the question to say what you already prepared, looks a little different: 'We downtrodden women **must** have a strong leader who will fight for our cause day and night. Men are dominant and arrogant — there was one in the paper yesterday, for example, who kept his wife in a dog kennel . . .'

Spot the difference?

Before going on . . .

Dress and looks
This is less important than you think. Sure, people look at you on TV, but then people look at you in the street or on the bus. Most people dress the way they want others to see

them. Do you look in the mirror in the morning when you dress? If so, you are already preparing yourself to go in front of the cameras.

So wear what you feel at your best in, what you want others to see you in. Preferably look smart. The main thing is to feel at home in your clothes. If you wear a suit to work, wear one to the studio.

There are, however, just a few tiny technicalities:

1. Don't wear stripes or checks — particularly narrow ones; they have a stroboscopic effect and appear to be moving.
2. Equally disconcerting is flashing jewellery, tie-pins, etc.
3. Keep off clashing or really loud colours (especially red). Colour is easily distorted on television and can make you look weird.
4. Almost black and off-white are OK (a bit drab, perhaps) but *never* wear straight black and white. It sends colour cameras bananas and makes you look grotesque.
5. Take a quick check in the mirror before going on. If you want to appear a straightforward, decent sort of person — which 99 per cent of interviewees should — then it does not pay to display things like stray hair, slipped tie knots, lopsided brassières and smudged mascara. The make-up people in most studios take care this doesn't happen, but it is amazing how many times people manage to appear looking like they have just been pulled through a hedge.

Transport to the studios
Often the studio will send a car for you, in which case the onus is on them to get you there in time. If they can't manage a car, then get a taxi or go by chauffeured car. Only drive there yourself as a last resort; it will take up vital extra minutes finding the place and parking.

Be absolutely certain in advance where the studios are. Many TV companies have studios all over the place, and nothing is guaranteed to cause disaster more certainly than arriving late, or even at the wrong place. Plan to arrive at the studio in plenty of time — at least a quarter of an hour early.

Final touches to brief

Having prepared your brief, condensed it and memorized it, what you now do with it is up to you. It is probably best to avoid the two extremities of either (a) throwing it away or (b) going to the studios clutching a mountain of papers.

My preference is for a small transparent folder containing a few relevant papers and the final version of the brief. Then on top of the pile goes what is virtually a laundry list of the points to be got over, with the really key points marked with a red dot from a felt-tip pen.

There are differing schools of thought on whether or not to use your notes in the studio, and if so, how to use them. This is discussed in more detail in 'Winning the battle', but for inveterate note-clutchers like me those red dots are invaluable. There is no time at all actually to *read* your notes during an interview, so the dots (kept to a minimum) help the eye to zap in on a vital point at an awkward moment.

Example of a final brief

X TV 'Look Round'
Vegetarian Interview
Interviewer — Cliff Hanger

1. Vegetables better and cheaper
   — ½ price of meat (wife . . . shopping)
   — all protein requirements
   — healthier — roughage
   (example of a fit vegetarian)
   — grow them in own garden (fun!)

2. Why animal foods bad
   — cholesterol (dead friend Joe)
   — impurities (fertilizer poisons)
   — bad for teeth

3. Ecological
   — increasing human population
   (500 new humans born during this interview)
   — decreasing animals
   — suffering
      — rearing conditions (describe calf in pen)
      — slaughtering conditions (describe slaughterhouse)

CHECK-LIST

PREPARATION

1. Decide whether to do it or not. Ask them:
   - ☐ when?
   - ☐ where?
   - ☐ how long?

2. Decide:
   - ☐ are you available?
   - ☐ do you want to do it?

   Weigh up the plus and minus points, but be inclined to answer 'yes'.

3. Ring them back. You'll want to know:
   - ☐ why are they doing this programme?
   - ☐ why me?
   - ☐ who is the interviewer?
   - ☐ will it be live or recorded?
   - ☐ any films or props?
   - ☐ who else will be on the programme?
   - ☐ what questions will they ask?

4. Prepare — at least an hour.
   - ☐ Say what *you* want to say, not what *they* want you to say.
   - ☐ Plan the message:
     - — 3 points (distil them; time is short) supported by
     - — 3 or 4 subpoints each.
   - ☐ Use:
     - — anecdotes. Tell it in stories.
     - — analogies. Ring a bell in the viewer's mind.
   - ☐ Learn your brief — parrot fashion. Then you will always have *something* to say.

5. Anticipate their angle. Likely questions can be deduced from:
   - ☐ what they said they would ask.
   - ☐ putting yourself in their shoes.   *(continued)*

36

CHECK-LIST *(continued)*

6. Remember — keep off the defensive. You are going
   to use *their* questions to get over *your* message.

DRESS AND APPEARANCE
☐ Be your presentable self.
☐ Avoid narrow stripes and checks.
☐ Avoid flashing jewellery etc.
☐ Never wear black and white.
☐ Check at last moment for stray hair, etc.

5. The television studio and what to expect

Reception

Many egos are deflated when they arrive at a television studio. After the preparation and build-up, it is a degrading experience to arrive at the studios and find that the girl on the desk (a) is occupied with some other call or visitor when you arrive, (b) has never heard of you, (c) does not know that you are expected by a production team and are about to broadcast to millions, and (d) couldn't really care if you went up in flames.

It's not that the receptionist is rude — simply that she deals with hundreds of people a day in a building where things are chaotic to a degree which no self-respecting company would tolerate. Soon, however, someone from the production team will come and collect you, and you will be looked after, though no one can expect VIP handling. Then, after a bewildering trip through corridors like the bowels of a ship, the next stop is usually the Green Room.

The 'Green Room'

This term has come down from the theatre, where it refers to the bare, seedy, airless room which acts as a buffer zone for performers to and from their hour of strutting and fretting on the stage.

Fortunately TV companies see the Green Room as a much more important place. There are usually comfortable chairs, a TV set for monitoring the programmes, and a well-stocked drinks cabinet.

The Green Room can be a fascinating place. People from all walks of television life come and go — famous faces, newscasters, presenters, producers, studio staff. It's a good baptism to the world of television and still performs its old theatrical role as a decompression chamber to adjust the body and mind for the next stage.

Maybe in one corner a fellow victim is getting the once-over from his interviewer and producer before going on. The door bursts open and a face known to millions, still scowling from a duff newscast, appears and only smiles again after making a bee-line for the drinks cabinet and pouring itself the right side of three fingers of gin.

Your time in the Green Room will depend on how long there is to go before your interview. You might have to spend half an hour there or you might not see it at all. It's also quite common, depending on schedules, to go back afterwards, when a friendly outfit will often play back the interview on a monitor.

Meet the interviewer
This is a good time to ask to see your interviewer and producer if possible — to go over the ground. This is important. Interviewers are usually anxious to meet their subjects and talk about the interview in broad terms, but don't take 'no' for an answer the first time if at this stage they tell you that you can't see your interviewer until he is throwing the first question.

OK, sometimes the interviewer will be so busy he can't get away, but you owe it to yourself to insist on seeing him.

What do you talk about? Ask again about the *line* of questions. He will usually give you an idea, because by now he has an idea of what he's going to ask. Like you, he's not going into the studio intending to play it by ear. Most times he'll tell you and most times he'll try to stick to it, but there are two traps to watch for:

1. He has a perfect right during the interview to ask something completely different. It may be something you say, it may be sudden inspiration on his part, or maybe he is trying to catch you out, but it's all in the rules. Hence the stuff earlier about anticipating questions but not relying on them wholesale.
2. It's a good idea at this stage to talk about your side of things — *but not too much*. The aim should be to ensure that the interviewer knows what you're about, so that

39

crossed wires are avoided and the interview has more
purpose. But most people have an overwhelming
temptation to talk at length about the points they want
to make, the questions they'd like to be asked and how
they intend to answer them. This is two-edged. It can
sometimes stimulate the interviewer into thinking 'Yes,
that's interesting, I must ask that.' But more often it can
smack of being a hobby-horse and cause him not to ask
you that question at any cost.

Unguarded talk

This desire to tell all to the interviewer in advance stems from
a deadly tendency to want to off-load on someone when
under stress. You know those Gestapo films: first the beatings
and torture, then the relaxed chat with a friendly 'doctor'
who offers you a cigarette and gets you to confide in him.
He's the 'soft' interrogator, and that's what television people
become in the Green Room or studio before a broadcast.
It's not usually deliberate on their part, but more beans are
spilled before interviews than during them.

Watch for the warning signs. Listen for yourself saying:
☐ 'Actually, this isn't in my notes, but . . .'
☐ 'I'm not going to say this in the studio, but . . .'
☐ 'I shouldn't really tell you this, but . . .'
☐ 'This is off the record, but . . .'

Nothing is off the record. There is no law, written or
unwritten, whereby even the kindest interviewer can't drag
up some whispered confidence and throw it straight back at
you, live, in front of the cameras.

So the simple rule is to be friendly, talk about your
subject by all means, joke, chat, but *never,* at *any* time,
before, during or after the show, in the Green Room, white
room, black room or bathroom, say *anything* to *anybody*
that you might afterwards regret.

Drinking

The trouble with alcohol is that it's pleasant stuff and relaxes
the nervous system. It can't be denied that a couple of drinks
before a programme can unwind you, but who said anything
about being unwound? That's just what you *don't* want to
be. *They* would love to have you sitting back in your chair,

relaxed, smiling amiably, coming out with a few witticisms and occasionally opening the cupboard door ever such a tiny bit for a quick peek at the skeleton.

To hell with what *they* want. *You* want to be alert, articulate, on the ball. People think it's impossible, but you can film the most seasoned drinker before and after a small drink and there is a marked deterioration in clarity and concentration to be seen in the second film. Drinks are best left till after the interview when you can drink the cabinet dry if they'll let you, so long as you still keep the lid on those secrets (and there's no danger of them wanting to do a retake just as you're cracking your third bottle!).

Nerves
The craving for a stiff drink at this stage is enhanced by the fact that you're shaking like a leaf. At least, you should be. If you don't experience that slight breathlessness and inverted stomach then it is time to start worrying, because over-confidence can be lethal.

Almost everybody, including seasoned interviewers, feel some tension before going on, and for a first-timer it is usually petrifying.

Good. Don't fight it. *Use* it.

Many experts recommend things like yoga, deep breathing, transcendental meditation and other tricks. But all that adrenalin is useful stuff. It makes you alert, lively, punchy, and it's a shame to lose it.

In the minutes before a boxer goes into a fight he's a bundle of nerves, but the moment the bell goes the nerves vanish. A television interview is just like that. Be a little masochistic for once and learn to enjoy the tension and use it to your advantage. In short doses it's good for you and makes a change from the humdrum of business, housework, the daily routine.

Make-up
Shortly before the programme you will be made up to prevent the cameras doing horrible things to you. Make-up experts are well used to nervous customers and are good value for a friendly chat. They know what they're doing and are best left to pat powder on your cheeks and put hair in place. Of course, if it looks like you are being transformed into Count

Dracula then say so, but you should find make-up a nice little interlude.

You're on next!

From make-up they will either lead you straight into the studio or back to the Green Room for a few minutes. Either way ... *you're on next!*

CHECK-LIST

☐ Ask to meet the interviewer — and producer if possible — to discuss the *line* of questions.
☐ Let him know what you're about, but don't give too much away.
☐ No confidences; *never* anything 'off the record'.
☐ Stay off the booze.
☐ Enjoy that nervous feeling. Use it to your advantage.

---

6. Winning the battle

Sorry about the military terms. But in a way it *is* a battle —
with yourself, with them, with anyone who disagrees with
your cause or your business.

The terrain

The battleground is the studio.

It looks more like a nuclear war has occurred — chaos
reigns. Technicians beaver away with cables, plugs, filters
and things. People rush around with clipboards and shout
instructions at each other. There are bright lights, cameras,
microphones. And in the middle of it all is a small oasis of
calm — the seats where you and your interviewer are to slug
it out.

Who does what

Editors, producers, directors, floor managers, researchers,
cameramen, secretaries, not to mention deputies and
assistants to them all — it's not worth worrying at this stage
about who's in charge. It varies from country to country
and from programme to programme.

It is fairly safe to assume that the person making the most
noise *between* takes is the producer, while the one making
all the noise *during* takes is the director. It's best to
intercede through the interviewer if you need anything.

This applies to all the distractions like clapper boards and
people making masonic-looking signs at the interviewer to
tell him that he's got ten seconds before take-off or that the
programme ended five minutes ago.

Let *them* do the worrying. If they want you to do anything they'll soon ask you. If you want anything just ask the interviewer.

Take your seats

Again, let *them* show you to your seat and do all the fussing. For the technician who slings the microphone round your neck, or clips it to your lapel, nothing is more infuriating than a fumbling interviewee trying to assist.

The only thing you need to fuss with once you've sat down (and I promise this will be the last military analogy) is a final check of your 'uniform'; a quick touch over the head and across the forehead for stray hair, tie straight and up into the collar, shirt straight. Pull the back of your coat down to stop it riding up behind the collar.

Now, *sit forward.* Perch on the edge of the chair if possible. The difference is staggering. If you sit in this slightly tense position you *feel* alert and, more important, you *look* alert throughout the interview.

Voice test

You know how maddening it is when you have to keep changing the volume control on your set? Some nights you wouldn't believe it, but in fact the studio has someone doing the 'sound mixing', in other words, trying to make everything leave the studio within a certain volume range.

They ask you to do a 'voice test' by saying a few words to see what your voice does to the needles on the sound mixer's console. Their favourite is to ask what you had for breakfast or lunch.

Here's a chance to make them happy right from the start. Virtually everybody either booms out their voice test and then starts the interview *sotto voce,* or they whisper the voice test and then launch into the first question like Billy Graham at a revivalist meeting. The former loses you the first few words while the mixer turns the volume up, and the latter makes millions of TV sets shudder while he frantically turns it down.

So give the voice test the same impact as you intend to use during the interview. The director and sound mixer will be delighted.

Good side/bad side

We're almost ready to start. First, though, it's important to think about how the viewer sees you. The horrible truth is that if he doesn't like your manner anything you say will be lost. All of us tend to be put off by someone who looks slick, shifty, scruffy or stupid on the screen.

It has nothing to do with being handsome or ugly. In fact the smooth looker often starts at a disadvantage.

It's all to do with the subtle difference between looking alert and looking nervous, between endearing mannerisms and infuriating tics, pausing for emphasis and gaping open-mouthed, appearing a 'character' and looking crazy.

For one thing, almost everyone has one profile that is more pleasing to the eye than the other. Look at photos of yourself, look in the mirror (preferably between two mirrors placed so as to give an accurate image), ask your relatives and close friends. It's not vanity to try to show the 'good' side to the cameras — it's an intelligent way of giving the best impression you can.

Of course, don't spoil the interview by thinking of nothing other than which side of your face the cameras are pointing at, but if you can develop a feel for your best image it will go some way towards winning over the viewer.

Where to look

Forget the cameras and look at the interviewer. If you try to look into the camera during an interview it appears contrived, and besides, you stand an even chance of looking into the wrong camera. A red light on top of the camera lights up when it is on, but even experienced newscasters often play Russian roulette between the red lights. There is no way of knowing when the director will order a different camera to cut in.

So *look at the interviewer*. Talk to the *interviewer* and you're talking to the *viewer*.

Speech

Forget the old 'rain in Spain' stuff. The only thing to remember is that your voice is going through all sorts of electronic gadgetry before hitting the ears of someone not accustomed to the way you speak. So speak *clearly* and distinctly — a little slowly if you're a fast talker — but

45

otherwise in your normal voice.

If you have a strong regional accent it's a *plus point*. Don't hide it. If it's good enough for a president of the USA, it's good enough for you.

Gestures
The days of sitting on your hands went out decades ago. If you want to wag an accusing finger at the interviewer, do so. If you feel like turning your palms up and saying 'My life, what a question!', go ahead. The only things to avoid are fussy or nervous movements. This goes for:

Mannerisms
A quick scratch on top of the head, rubbing an eye, cleaning a pair of spectacles are really quite human. They can even be used to good effect. For instance, a genteel blowing of the nose can give you five seconds of vital thinking time in a tight spot (ten, if you carefully fold the handkerchief and put it away).

Again, though, beware of nervy and irritating habits. Don't drum the table, fiddle with paper-clips or bite your nails. Cameramen are always on the lookout, by way of a break from routine, for a prime minister picking his nose in an unguarded moment or a lady senator scratching behind a bra-strap.

Smoking
No. Definitely no. A lot of people do smoke in the studio, but it is distracting, slovenly and messy. Those wisps of smoke floating across the screen can be infuriating. And strange things can happen. In one interview (fortunately it was in a training session), the subject lit a cigarette half-way through. He did so while the camera was on the interviewer, so the viewer had no indication that a cigarette had suddenly appeared on the scene. The subject took an enormous drag on his cigarette, and at that moment the camera cut back to him, in close-up, for an answer to the interviewer's question.

The effect was extraordinary. This apparently normal man, half-way through a successful interview, opened his mouth to speak and belched out smoke like Puff the Magic Dragon. The smoke poured out. It came out of his mouth and nostrils. It even seemed to come out of his ears. His otherwise excellent answer — and the rest of the interview, for that matter — was lost for ever on a hysterical audience.

Pipes are OK, but *only* if (a) you are an experienced pipeman and it's part of your image, and (b) you don't light the wretched thing — or at least don't emit smoke. Used properly, a pipe is good for buying thinking time or pointing accusingly at the interviewer.

Smiling

Some say do, some say don't. On balance smiles should be treated with caution. For one thing, they can make you seem a big smug, and there is always the danger, in a recorded interview, of the edited tape or film showing your cheerful, smiling face just after an edited-in serious question or accusation. Appearing to beam from ear to ear when asked your opinion of an earthquake in Peru is not guaranteed to enamour you to the viewer.

However, it's not worth worrying about too much. A naturally cheerful person should not be prevented from smiling, and a naturally sour type certainly shouldn't use his first TV interview to learn to grin.

Notes

Lastly, there's the question of what to do with your notes. People have more hang-ups about it than most other aspects of interviewing or public speaking. There is no reason on earth why you shouldn't have a notepad on your knee or in front of you on the table. It can actually give you quite a professional look, especially if it conveys the impression of your being armed with plenty of facts and figures.

The great big golden rule is *not to read from them*. By all means produce a relevant document and wave it around, or refer to a table of figures or something, but if the camera catches you peering at your notes in a frantic search for the answer to the last question, then you have blown the interview. You just won't seem credible to the viewer any more.

Hence those headings and red dots in the brief. With any luck, if you prepared properly, you can look the interviewer in the eye throughout because it's all in your head. But if you get stuck, then you can give yourself a prompt with no more than a quick glance.

Sincerity

The last, and most important thing, is to be *sincere* and *enthusiastic* throughout.

Horror story

So much for the preliminaries. Let's get started on the interview.

Suddenly, it's all about to happen for real. A voice calls out '30 seconds' — and you and the interviewer stop talking and look at each other like two waxwork dummies for what seems an eternity.

Then he speaks, and the cameras are recording.

Your head is now on the block. In the next few minutes it is in your power to promote yourself, your company or your cause to immense advantage. Or you can make an utter fool of yourself. It's up to you.

Let's now create a victim and look at a duff interview. The characters and every aspect of the script are borrowed from what happens in real life — from different interviews at different times, in different words. Though fictional, our interview is certainly not impossible.

We have a typical interviewee — a businessman — and a typical interviewer. They are male only for convenience, and a businessman has been selected as one of the vast group of people who are likely to be asked to do an interview, yet who have the least experience in television techniques. But the things we are about to see — the questions, the tricks, the pitfalls, the missed opportunities — apply to us all, male, female, of all ages and walks of life.

The story so far

Will E Makit is chief executive of Basket Eggs, a big poultry and egg producer. The company has announced plans to build a plant at Foxtooth, a town of 100,000 inhabitants. It will be one of the biggest companies in the region, and the local TV station has brought Makit in to be interviewed on the evening current affairs programme.

The interviewer, Cliff Hanger, is a seasoned pro. In real life he's a nice guy, with a wife and four children. He holds doors open for old ladies in supermarkets and feeds the ducks on a Sunday afternoon. But he's a bit cynical about businessmen and has one fault; if he thinks someone is a baddie, or is trying to pull a fast one on him, he goes in for the kill.

He's told Makit about his line of questioning, but has been pretty vague — 'What will the factory do?', 'How much will it cost?', 'Any particular problems?', etc.

Makit, for his part, is completely confident about the interview. There's nothing he doesn't know about chickens, he's a good after-dinner speaker and his wife thinks he's handsome. He's so calm about it, in fact, that he got in a quick nine holes at the local golf-course before going to the studios.

It's 6.30 pm, and the interview is going out live. Hanger launches into his introduction.

Here's the script. Most of the studio directions are omitted for simplicity, and the numbers are inserted for reference when we analyse the interview afterwards. Read it through in one go before going back through the numbers.

Hanger: Our next guest on the programme is someone who has a lot to answer for. He's Will E Makit *(cut to Makit, sitting back (1), smiling, arms folded)* who's to build a poultry plant on the outskirts of Foxtooth. The type of plant planned is to be like the one in this film. *(Film: 45 seconds, showing rearing of chicks and battery conditions, some birds dying, most losing feathers etc) (2).* Mr Makit, why are you bringing this kind of thing to Foxtooth?

Makit: *(3)* Well, it's a logical decision. The company is expanding and Foxtooth is an ideal location for a new poultry plant. In fact...

Hanger: *(4)* But we've just seen how senseless suffering is caused to countless thousands of chickens. Why not buy a field here and let them fly around a bit?

Makit: *(5)* Ah, that simply wouldn't be economical, Cliff *(6).* On a free-range basis you need a square-footage-to-bird ratio of 14.7:1 on grade A feed, and more on lower quality grain *(7).*

Hanger: Are you saying that you practically torture helpless birds, simply because it's more profitable that way?

Makit: Well, it's hardly torture *(8).* I'm just saying that all the people watching this programme... *(9)*

Hanger: We all know, though, that your method produces lower quality eggs *(4).* In the film they showed a waste-burning unit; are you going to bring one of those here?

Makit: *(5)* Oh yes. That's standard equipment in this sort of plant.

Hanger: But that chimney in the film was belching filthy black smoke over the neighbourhood. Now you're telling us that we're to have a factory chimney polluting the atmosphere *(10).*

Makit: Well *(11)* I should like to reassure the viewers that the

chimney will only produce about 120,000 cubic feet of waste
smoke per hour *(pause) (12)*. And it won't be burning all the
time, of course *(pause)*. I mean, you can't run a plant of this
sort without some waste smoke *(pause)*. Besides, er . . . *(13)*
(pause) this sort of production requires a certain amount of
recycling and waste-burning and so on *(14)*.

Hanger: All the same, 120,000 cubic feet sounds like an awful lot of
black smoke for a small town like Foxtooth. Tell me, Mr Makit,
how long is the plant going to take to build?

Makit: Just under a year, we hope, though the first eggs should be in
production on a limited scale within nine months. We've got
a really good firm on the job, and once it's finished it'll be
the most modern plant of its kind.

Hanger: Who's building the plant for you then?

Makit: I . . . *(15)* Why do you want to know? *(16)*

Hanger: It would be interesting to know if it's a local firm. The
construction industry round here has been going through a
rough patch lately, hasn't it?

Makit: Has it? *(17)* I must admit I'm not using a local firm . . .

Hanger: Why not?

Makit: Well, quite simply because we've chosen Stackbricks to do
the job.

Hanger: Why Stackbricks, though?

Makit: Well . . . I mean . . . *(angrily) (18)* look, why are you asking
me all this stuff about the builders? You're making me sound
as though I've been bribed or something! *(19)*

Hanger: *(coolly)* OK, so it's a year from now and you've built the
factory. What benefit are we going to get out of it?

Makit: Well, the great advantage of the Makit system is that you get
more eggs for less money. Everything is automatic so we can
cut costs and provide a cheaper egg by the thousand.

Hanger: I see. Do you have enough eggs for export, then?

Makit: Oh yes! We even sell frozen eggs to the People's Republic of
China!

Hanger: I'm glad to hear it. That's Mr Will E Makit, who's going to build
a plant here to send eggs to China. What the people of Foxtooth
will do for eggs is anybody's guess *(20) (cut)*.

The lessons to be learnt

That interview took just over two minutes. In that time our
friend Mr Makit put his foot in it at least 20 times.

OK, so the interview is a fictional one. Interviewers are
not always as vicious as Hanger, and interviewees not always
as dumb as Makit. But many of those 20 points will crop up
even in the kindest interview and, when you get the
occasional tough one, all 20 will be dotted over the
interview like land-mines.

Let's go back over the interview, point by point, and see why

Mr Makit *didn't* make it. All the points are important, but six are golden rules (numbers *4, 5, 7, 8, 9* and *16*).

(1) LOOK ALERT
It's terribly tempting to try to relax in a studio chair. This can make you look too contented — if not a complete slob. It's especially true if the opening gambit is an attack on you; the camera catches you sitting back, smiling smugly, and the viewer already wants to see the interviewer wipe that silly smile right off your face.

(2) ANY SURPRISES?
Remember back in the preparation you asked if they were showing any film? If they *are* using film you should insist on seeing it first. The same applies to surprise studio guests and any other gimmicks.

(3) SHOUT 'UNFAIR'
If they say it's impossible, or say there's no film and then spring it on you anyway, you must let the viewer know right away that *you* haven't seen the bit of film which *he's* just seen.

Sometimes they will even show film without your being able to see it on a studio monitor during the interview, in which case you must be doubly sure to let the viewer know all about this mean trick.

If your interview was recorded, and they then use film to your disadvantage, it's time to complain. (More on that soon.)

(4) DON'T LET THE INTERVIEWER BUTT IN
In normal conversation we tend to stop when someone butts in. On television the reverse applies. *You* hold the whip hand, because there's nothing they hate more in the studio than two people talking at once.

If the interviewer cuts in before you've finished, *raise your voice — slightly but firmly — and finish what you were saying.* He'll have to shut up or ruin the interview.

However, don't confuse making your point with waffle. *Always* finish the point you were making and then shut up. *Never* go rabbitting on for more than about 15 seconds at a time.

(5) REFUTE INCORRECT STATEMENTS
What kind of a question was that? Here Hanger is using the oldest trick in the book — a derogatory statement followed by a different question. It's a favourite trick, so be on your guard for it. If the interviewer makes any statement that you don't like, jump in and put the record straight *immediately*. Then answer the question.

(6) NO NAMES
It's a small point, but don't forget that you're not talking to the *interviewer* — you're talking to the *viewer*. If you address him by name it removes you one stage from the person with whom you want to communicate.

Be especially careful of first names. They can make the interview sound a bit contrived or 'pally'.

(7) NO JARGON
That spiel about the 14.7:1 ratio may look ludicrous, but it happens all the time. People are so used to the gobbledygook of their everyday jobs that they forget the viewer can't understand a word of it.

Remember instead the advice in the briefing chapter about using simple analogies. (Example: a space expert in a recent interview explaining the nature and dimensions of the Russian Soyuz space station: 'It fits together like a child's construction set. With the latest addition it's now about the size of a domestic garage.')

(8) DON'T DEFEND
Somehow on television it's as bad as an admission of guilt. *He* used the word 'torture': now *you've* used the same word again, which is just what he wanted.

Either go straight into your (already prepared) point about the benefits of battery breeding or, if you have to reiterate his loaded question, use it as a launching pad for a counter-attack.

(9) THERE IS ONLY ONE VIEWER
He is an individual. He is not 'one' or the 'audience' or the 'viewer'. You are speaking to him through the interviewer and it shouldn't be necessary to refer to him as anyone in particular — not even as 'you' (except in a straight-to-camera talk).

Picture yourself in an *average* television-viewing mood. Even intelligent people tend to switch off mentally when they watch, and then you must allow for the fact that a typical audience covers the whole spectrum of education and taste, with the weighting towards the lower end of the scale.

A good tip is to think of someone you know in real life who to you is an average person in the street. It might be your mother, husband, wife, cleaning lady, postman or teenage offspring. Throughout the interview picture that person standing there in place of the nearest camera. You continue talking to Cliff Hanger, but really the person you want to get through to is that individual where the camera is.

(By now we can see that some numbers have repeated themselves. Alas, there's no law to stop you making the same mistake over and over.)

(10) DON'T LET THEM MISINTERPRET
Another popular trick is to paraphrase your message for you. It's often done with good intentions to achieve simplicity, and if young Hanger has just put it better than you can put it yourself, then so much the better.

But if it's done to your detriment, put it straight at once.

(11) WELL...
It's human nature to start with a 'Well . . .' It doesn't do any harm in small doses, but that's the third time Makit's started with 'Well' in five questions. He's losing impact.

(12) THE CALCULATED PAUSE
It's like when you put your foot in it at a party and want the floor to open up. You ask some lady how her husband is these days, and remember as you speak that he died last month. So you quickly burble some other nonsense to cover up and realize you're saying something worse.

The interviewer loves it. He loves it so much, in fact, that he won't always wait for you to say something stupid in the first place. He'll create a pregnant silence for you to fill — like your own grave. Watch for yourself how often a subject on television goes on talking because he feels he has to.

Yet here's a situation where you really hold the whip hand.

Say what you want to say . . . then shut up. The interviewer
is only too conscious that if his interview is filled with long
pauses he'll be chewed out by the producer for a boring
piece. The onus is on *him* to keep things flowing. If he clams
up suddenly and deliberately, be sure you've got one of your
key points over, then sit there in silence and wait for him to
crack. He will.

(13) ER, UM
It's worth some practice in everyday speech. The more you
'um' and 'er' and 'ah', the less certain you sound of your facts.

(14) AND SO ON AND SO FORTH AND THE LIKE
Meaningless. List your items and quit while you're ahead.

(15) HE WHO HESITATES IS SERVED UP ON TOAST
This may sound contradictory·having just encouraged you to
shut up in certain circumstances, and having talked earlier
of ploys like cleaning your spectacles and blowing your nose
in order to gain thinking time. But the crucial thing is not to
let the *viewer* know that you're frantically thinking up the
right answer! Stall intelligently if you have to, or launch
straight into your response.

Incidentally, quite a good breathing-space technique is to
ask the interviewer to repeat the question (though obviously
it would look ridiculous after a simple question like the one
about the builders).

In fact in this particular case Hanger's question is a
sidetrack, and right now Makit shouldn't be answering the
question at all, as we shall see.

(16) DON'T BE SIDETRACKED
Interviewers are always looking for a dark alley-way with a
corpse at the end of it. (This is one reason for not relying too
much on prepared questions and answers.)

A good interviewer can sniff trouble a mile away at the
end of a sidetrack. If you give him half a chance he'll be off
down it like a frustrated ferret — so it's your job to keep him
on the main street.

The question of who's building the plant is of immense
local interest, though you can see that Hanger hadn't thought
of it — he got the lead accidentally from Makit ('We've got a

really good firm on the job . . .').

From Makit's point of view it's a dangerous sidetrack and he compounds the danger for the next three questions before he spots what's happening.

It's a tricky one, this. Some successful interviewees, particularly politicians, escape by simply not answering the question, but in this case the local viewer will soon realize that Makit's hiding something if he evades the question altogether.

He'll have to give a quick answer and belt back into the main street again. Let's see if we can get him out of it when we redo the interview in a few moments.

(17) KNOW YOUR GROUND
It should go without saying. Interviewers are usually backed up by research teams who ply them with facts and figures. If you *are* caught out, don't make it worse with a dumb retort like 'Has it?'

(18) STAY COOL
Never lose your temper. If you ever became really adept at being interviewed you might *pretend* to show great anger and indignation at the right moment, but that's outside the range of this simple book.

Stay as cool and professional as you can. Once you become ruffled the interviewer is half-way to the kill.

(19) DON'T VOLUNTEER THINGS
Makit has just done exactly what Hanger wanted him to do. Hanger knew he would be in hot water if he himself made any allegations of corruption, so he's let Makit imply the allegations himself.

We do it all the time in conversation — it's another of those crazy defence mechanisms. On the air it's as good as a confession of guilt.

(20) THE LAST WORD
Another favourite. See for yourself how often it happens. Under the guise of 'winding up', the interviewer delivers the *coup-de-grâce* while you sit there open-mouthed and the clock ticks to zero.

In recorded interviews the detrimental, snide final comment

is sometimes edited into the end, in which case it's an occasion for a complaint (we'll look at complaints later).

In a live interview, however, you again hold the whip hand if he slips in a derogatory remark, because you can utterly ruin his summary by shouting out and getting your case in last.

But you have to be damned quick. Come out with something like: 'That isn't true. I've already told you that xyz . . .', so that they finally cut the interview with you reiterating one of your key points.

One television trainer tells his students: 'If you can't think of anything else, at least shout "Rubbish!" as loud as you can. It's better than saying nothing.'!

The key points

I deliberately saved Makit's first and biggest mistake till now. *He went in cold, without a brief.* He failed to hammer any key points home — because he didn't have any key points to hammer home in the first place.

He made the cardinal error of playing the interview by ear because he thought he had all the answers in his head.

Now, for a spot of practice, why not go over Makit's interview and look for the main points he *should* have got over?

He wants to make it clear that Basket Eggs is good news. What are the positive points?

1. For a start, it must be demonstrable that eggs are beneficial or presumably one wouldn't eat so many of the things. This is a great time for Makit to be selling his product — to make the viewer want to go out and buy a dozen.
2. Secondly, a major investment in plant can be shown to be a benefit to the community. Basket Eggs is sure to provide jobs, to add to the income from rates and to boost local trade.
3. And then there's the fact that mass production should make for *cheaper* eggs — that's good news for the housewife.

Of course, there are other points — those valuable exports to China, for example. But Makit should major on no more than two or three main points. The viewer simply can't absorb any more. Other points can be slipped in if there's time.

It's worth noting, from these three points alone, how quickly you can start to spot some of Hanger's irresistible nasties in advance. For example: there are plenty of experts who say eggs are bad for you; there's the fact that a new plant will destroy some piece of greenery; and what about those poor old hens?

In any case Makit should have come to terms long ago with the negative aspects of his business. It would be wrong to pretend that everything's perfect in business, and Makit's line of work is full of warts which it would be both immoral and impractical to try to hide. His job here is to highlight the good bits and play down the negative ones.

Getting the message over

Shortly we will rerun the interview and see if Makit could have got those key points over despite Hanger's loaded questions.

And here we come to the most important point of all: *you can make your points regardless of the questions.*

It's incredibly simple. There isn't a question in the world that you can't turn to your advantage.

Every question is nothing more than a peg for you to hang your case on. There are varying degrees. Some questions are 'gifts' and enable you to say what you wanted to say simply by answering the question. Most questions, however, require some kind of answer before getting on to your own material. Only as a very last resort should a question be ignored completely.

The principle of what it's all about is summed up by a real-life statement in a television interview by a trade union leader: 'Let me answer *my* questions first and then I'll answer *yours!*'

It may be taking things a bit far to put it in those words on the air, but that's the thought which should always be at the back of your mind.

The best way is to answer the question *briefly* and then move on to your own material. Let's say, for example, that Hanger throws in a question about production: 'Just how many eggs a day will your plant produce?' A fair enough question. But Makit's first key point had nothing to do with the number of eggs; it was to tell the viewer that eggs are good for him and that he should eat more. He knows his plant will produce 50,000 eggs a day — now all he has to do is to add a bit: 'Fifty thousand. That's 50,000 meals. One egg alone has enough protein and vitamins to keep you going for half a day.'

Well, Cliff Hanger is a seasoned pro and knows propaganda when he sees it, so he quickly changes tack: 'According to some experts, eggs can cause heart failure — is this what you're advocating?'

But Makit hasn't finished selling his eggs. It would be a mistake to skip the heart failure problem altogether so he *uses* the question: 'Taken to excess, *anything* causes heart failure. But a couple of eggs a day are really good for you — and they're so versatile. They're delicious boiled, fried, scrambled and in omelettes.'

We caught a glimpse of this simple technique in the last chapter with our female liberationist friend who was asked about her qualifications for the job and *appeared* to answer the question with an attack on men.

It's something you can practise in your head, in three simple stages:

1. Think of something you'd like to say if you were given 15 seconds of free television time.
2. Think up the nastiest, most loaded, antipathetic question about the subject.
3. Put the two together!

Watch the pros doing it. Next time you see a politician getting away with murder, look for the techniques:

☐ 'Racial discrimination *is* a problem, I agree, and it has a bearing on what I was about to say . . .'
☐ 'I can't really answer that question without explaining some of the background . . .'
☐ 'Sure, some people say we made a mistake, but we mustn't let it cloud the real issue, which is . . .'
☐ 'That's a good question and I'd like to return to it later. But just to dwell for a moment on your earlier question about . . .'
☐ 'You're asking *me* about X. Let me ask *you* about Y . . .'

There is no limit to the number of ways you can use a

question for your own purposes. It's not like a court of law. There's no judge to rap his gavel and say 'Will you kindly answer the question!'

By the same token, though, there's nothing to stop the interviewer rephrasing the question and throwing it back at you later on. Good interviewers are like terriers. They'll keep on biting at the same heel. So, once you've got out of a tight corner, don't breathe a sigh of relief and mop your brow. Save that for after the programme.

Eventually, Hanger will have to give up because he knows it's dull television to keep on asking one question.

Remember, though, that *evading questions is just a technique for tight spots* and for getting your message over.

Too often, experienced performers find they enjoy evading questions so much that they do it all the time, just for the hell of it. Our friend the viewer may not realize what your game is the first few times, but you are eroding your credibility every time you refuse to strike a ball.

Let's say Hanger asks Makit how much profit he made last year. Makit knows he made a packet. And he knows Hanger knows it. This is a case for a 'perspective' answer, rather than evasion:

— 'Last year was an exceptionally good one, but let's get it in perspective. We made 30 million, but eggs are a highly risky business and with all the money we're putting into the Foxtooth plant we'll need all the cash we can get', or:
— 'It works out at a tenth of a penny per egg', or:
— 'At first sight it *looks* a lot — 50 million pre-tax in fact — but don't forget 20 million of that goes straight to the Government to provide schools, defence and welfare . . .'

(Incidentally, as sure as eggs is eggs, Hanger is only waiting for the *figure*. The moment Makit says 30 or 50 million, Hanger will leap in with: '*30 million!* Here you are making a killing while . . .' Don't let him get away with it. Keep talking and insist on making your point.)

Don't be afraid, either, of saying you can't answer a question if it's genuinely impossible. This is often the case during delicate strike negotiations, or where lives or official secrets are at stake. Say that you can't answer and briefly explain why. Then quickly return to one of your key points before the interviewer can open his mouth for the next question.

Success

Now it's time to apply the lessons to Makit's first interview. The story's the same. The people are the same, and to demonstrate how Makit should have dealt with each question we'll keep the questions the same:

Hanger: Our next guest on the programme is someone who has a lot to answer for. He's Will E Makit *(cut to Makit, sitting forward, intent and alert)* who's to build a poultry plant on the outskirts of Foxtooth. The type of plant planned is to be like the one in this film. *(Film: 45 seconds, showing rearing of chicks and battery conditions, some birds dying, most losing feathers etc)*

Hanger: Mr Makit, why are you bringing this kind of thing to Foxtooth?

Makit: *(1)* I can't comment on a film which I wasn't able to see myself *(2)*, but I trust it showed the immense improvement in the standards of egg production in the last few years. The Foxtooth plant . . .

Hanger: But we've just seen . . .

Makit: *(3) (more firmly)* The Foxtooth plant will give a vital boost to what is probably the most important area of food production today *(4)*.

Hanger: But we've just seen how senseless suffering is caused to countless thousands of chickens. Why not buy a field here and let them fly around a bit?

Makit: If you'd shown film of a field of chickens you'd see why *(5)*. Next time you see a flock of free-range chickens, just watch them for a while. Their life is hell. You'll see that a few strong birds peck the others into a state where they're so miserable that they lay far less eggs than their protected sisters in a battery plant *(6)*.

Hanger: Are you saying that you practically torture helpless birds, simply because it's more profitable that way?

Makit: *(7)* All the evidence points to the fact that our hens have a safer and longer life and lay more eggs *(8)*. We can check them the whole time so we know that every egg which leaves our plant is good and wholesome.

Hanger: We all know, though, that your method produces lower quality eggs. In the film they showed a waste-burning unit; are you going to bring one of those here?

Makit: *(9)* Listen, our eggs have been tested side-by-side with free-range eggs and they are every bit as good. Do you realize that there are more protein and nutrients in one single egg than in any other foodstuff at the price? *(10)*

Hanger: What about this waste-burning unit?

Makit: *(11)* Either you have a pile of chicken feathers a mile high or you burn them *(12)*. As a matter of fact our process has a number of useful side products — manure, chicken paste, offal.

Hanger: But that chimney in the film was belching filthy black smoke over the neighbourhood. Now you're telling us that we're to have a factory chimney polluting the atmosphere.

Makit: I'm telling you the exact opposite. I don't know what *your* film chimney was doing, but *ours* will produce no more smoke than half a dozen domestic chimneys *(13)* — and only sporadically at that.

Hanger: Tell me, Mr Makit, how long is the plant going to take to build?

Makit: The sooner the better as far as everyone's concerned! When this plant is in production it'll mean 200 new jobs for Foxtooth *(14)*. It's the biggest industrial investment in this region for years.

Hanger: Who's building the plant for you then?

Makit: *(15)* It's important first to look at the scope of the project. These new buildings will be the most up-to-date, safe and efficient in the world. We're investing a fortune to produce the best eggs at the lowest price.

Hanger: But it would be interesting to know if it's a local firm. The construction industry round here has been going through a rough patch lately, hasn't it?

Makit: *(16)* It has everywhere, I'm afraid, and of course we looked at the local building firms when we tendered. In this case we chose Stackbricks because of their experience of building this sort of plant. Next time you're in the Ducktown region, take a look at the big, modern egg farm they built there . . . *(17)*

Hanger: OK, so it's a year from now and you've built the factory. What benefit are we going to get out of it? *(18)*

Makit: *(19)* The biggest single benefit is that you'll get more eggs for less money. Everything is automatic so *we* can cut costs and give *you* a cheaper egg.

Hanger: I see. Do you have enough eggs for export, then?

Makit: Oh yes! We even sell frozen eggs to the People's Republic of China.

Hanger: I'm glad to hear it. That's Mr Will E Makit, who says he's going to build a plant here to send eggs to China. Meanwhile, I wonder what the people of Foxtooth will do for eggs.

Makit: *(20)* They come first, of course . . . *(cut)*

That's more like it

There's no such thing as a perfect interview, and that one won't go down in television history. But this time Makit made a good showing by applying some elementary techniques. With the same story and basically the same questions he got his key points over and dealt firmly with the nasty questions.

What's more, Hanger and his masters will be pleased with this more lively and informative interview, so the odds have improved on Makit being invited back for another go — when the factory opens, for example.

It's worth a look back over the interview to examine the ways Makit improved. This time he *scored* 20 times. We'll just run over the inserted numbers and see what lessons he learnt:

(1) He's making it clear to the viewer, right from the start, that he hasn't seen the film himself. Not only does this stop him making a fool of himself but it also encourages the viewer to side with Makit over this unfair treatment.

(2) Then he immediately uses the unseen film as a bridge to stress the improvements in egg production.

(3) No nonsense. He hadn't finished speaking so he beat Hanger at his own game and cut in. Note that he does so firmly rather than loudly. You shouldn't have to shout.

(4) We're still at the start of the interview, but Makit's now got two points in already. He's used the 'improvements' bit as a peg for reminding the viewer that eggs are an important food product.

(5) In the first interview he was on the defensive over this 'suffering' accusation. This time he attacks by comparing it with the apparently greater suffering of free-range chickens.

(6) And by now he's telling a *story* — painting a picture for the viewer of a lot of chickens giving each other a rough time.

(7) Hanger won't give in on his 'suffering' angle. So Makit uses it to reiterate his view that his chickens are happier.

(8) He also realizes, though, that Hanger is starting to sidetrack him with this 'suffering' angle. So, before Hanger can get started again, Makit bangs in another key point on the back of his 'happy hens' argument. He's starting to make the viewer feel like eating an egg.

(9) This is the nearest he gets to showing anger. Underneath he's furious at Hanger's sniping, but that 'listen . . .' is firm, not angry, and he's really telling the *viewer* 'listen to *me*, not *him*.'

(10) And again he uses the moment to sell a few more eggs.

(11) It doesn't take much imagination to convert a simple reassurance about a waste-burning unit into an image

in the viewer's mind of a pile of chicken feathers a mile
high. Yet it doubles the impact.

(12) 'And while we're on the subject of waste-burners', Makit
says in effect, 'look at all the other goodies you're going
to get out of my factory.' His plug for chicken paste
doesn't really have much to do with the waste-burner,
but it only takes a few words to link the two.

(13) Here's a good example of an analogy. Gone are the
120,000 cubic feet and in their place are half a dozen
domestic chimneys — which the viewer can picture
at once.

(14) It's taken a couple of minutes for Makit to have a
chance to get this key point in, but he's not going to
let it go. Again, he uses the question as a bridge. If he
merely answers the question 'How long is it going to
take to build?', he'll never demonstrate the boost he's
giving to employment in the region. The technique is
essential and *simple*, but it requires constant practice.

(15) Makit smells obvious trouble in the question about the
builders. It can only be trouble as there's no other
reason for asking a dumb question like that. So he
sidesteps the question, if a little crudely, and gets on
with another plug. But this time it doesn't work. It's a
reasonable attempt to evade the question, and he's
gained some thinking time, but he realizes that Hanger
isn't going to let this one go in a hurry.

(16) So this time he says who the builders are, but quickly
explains, honestly and rationally, the reason for the
choice. Note his first response, by the way. In fact he
doesn't know any more about the local construction
scene than he did in the first interview, but 'it has
everywhere, I'm afraid' shows much more apparent
understanding and sympathy than 'has it?'

(17) Now he's painting a picture for the viewer again and
starting, in effect, to describe what his new plant will
look like.

(18) There are times to forget the rules, and this is one of
them. OK, Hanger has interrupted again, but he also
happens to be changing the subject, which is just what
Makit wants. So this time he lets Hanger carry on.

(19) Don't look a gift horse in the mouth! It's quite easy to
be so much on the ball with interview techniques that

you overlook a chance to give a straight answer to a straight question.

(20) It's not much of a rejoinder but he's got to be quick. At least he points out that Foxtooth will get its eggs, and he spoils Hanger's snide little wind-up.

Just a few rules. A few techniques. All of them very simple. Yet with a bit of preparation and practice the same person achieves a 100 per cent improvement.

One thing which doesn't show in a script is *sincerity*. This time round Makit has scored several points, but it's important to avoid being smug or snide when winning. It can be tempting to sit back with a satisfied smile, but this must be avoided at all costs.

The important thing is to show the viewer that you're winning, not to show him that you *know* you're winning.

Sit still at the end

One last small point: many's the person who's finished an interview with an immense feeling of relief and blurted out something like 'Phew, I thought you had me there, Cliff!', only to find that the cameras are still live. Once the interview has been wound up, remain sitting, looking at the interviewer, until someone tells you it's over. Avoid the temptation to say anything or to jump up and walk out.

Complaints department

TV companies have quite strict codes of ethics. The recently produced 'Television Programme Guidelines' of Britain's Independent Broadcasting Authority are a case in point.

But there are rare occasions when they do the dirty on you.

As a general rule it's best to ride with the punches. It may be very satisfying to wring a grudging apology out of them for having asked a lot of loaded questions, but it won't undo the damage and will only create an even more unpleasant atmosphere.

It's the same as with unbalanced newspaper reports. In the long run it's usually bad PR to keep protesting at misrepresentation. The best advice is to forget the bad bits and work instead on getting better coverage next time.

However, there are times when enough is enough and a programme oversteps even the most generous bounds of journalistic licence. Then it is time to hit back, hard.

It should virtually never have to apply to *live* interviews. If they wipe the floor with you 'live' then you have only yourself to blame.

Even so, there are occasional exceptions, the most likely one being the interviewer's wind-up. No matter how quick you are, there are times when an interviewer will slip in a final cutting and incorrect remark before you can open your mouth. The sound cuts out and you're made to look a fool.

In cases where you have to complain, it's best to go for immediate retribution. Only you can know how good you are at showing your anger and putting people in their place, but your aim should be to make them run an immediate apology for what they've just done. But be absolutely certain that you have a *genuine* grievance.

One ploy is to refuse to leave your seat. This is especially effective if they need to use the studio for another interview — which they usually do. Say you're not going to shift until you've seen the producer, and when he appears say you're staying where you are until they've put out an apology and you've seen it on the monitor. (In fact it's enough to leave the studio as soon as they promise to apologize, but don't let them know that at first.)

If they simply pack up and leave you in an empty studio, get up and hound the producer, or if he refuses to talk, go and find the controller of programmes. Let it be quite clear that you're not bluffing and that until they (a) put out a correct statement and (b) apologize, you are going to make their lives hell.

If the crime occurred during a diary-type or news programme it's quite a simple matter for them to insert the apology during the same programme (unless yours was the last interview and the programme is just starting on the opening shots of *Star Wars*, in which case it will be better for you and them to do it at the first possible moment later in the day!).

The commonest character assassinations are perpetrated, however, in *filmed* interviews. With a bit of judicious editing the most brilliant performance can be turned into a disaster, and editors often have their reasons for horsing around with a piece of film.

Most commonly a filmed interview will be chopped around to achieve 'balance'. You might find yourself answering the last question early in the programme, then dealing with the first point at the end after extracts from other parts of the interview.

The editor or producer will frequently use only a brief extract from your interview, which will give the screened version a bias you hadn't intended. They will often add observations of their own after your appearance which you might have refuted if you'd been there to do so. Or they may take a statement of yours completely out of context and precede it with an edited-in comment.

It's always a shock when you sit eagerly in front of your set after a good interview and before your very eyes they show some seemingly irrational mutation of the original, and it will often be your first reaction to pick up the phone to ring your lawyer.

Again, however, this should really only be a last resort. The people who make TV programmes are hired and fired on their ability to present watchable material, and they deserve a fair amount of editorial leeway. What may seem like mindless tinkering to us is their expression of their art — for better or worse.

React according to the degree to which you've been misrepresented. In a filmed interview the *sense* may be changed by editing but the *impression* might well be satisfactory, in which case a quick shout at the producer may be the most you should do.

It's the same with rephrased questions. If only the words have been changed it's not worth complaining, but if the question itself has been radically altered then you shouldn't have to tolerate it.

But if you feel that you have been misrepresented you must stand up for your rights.

The first thing is to be sure of your facts. One tip is to take a small tape-recorder into the interview in the first place and to tape the screened version for comparison. It's also good policy to insist on seeing the final version before it goes out. If they're still editing as the signature tune goes out there's not much you can do about it, but there's no reason why you shouldn't see it if it's been edited in advance.

You can't *make* them show you the film, but they will often co-operate.

If a programme has gone out on the air and you *know* you've been wronged, here are the channels of complaint. If the first one fails to produce results, move up to the next authority, and so on:

1. *Producer/editor* — Immediate verbal complaint and demand redress.
2. *Controller of programmes* — Written complaint. Keep it factual. They are sensitive to criticism.
3. *Complaints board* — Written complaint. They take complaints *very* seriously. In Britain these are the BBC Programmes Complaints Commission, and the Complaints Review Board of the IBA.
4. *Lawyer* — As a very last resort . . . sue.

Self-assessment

The best complaints, however, are those you direct against yourself. Whether you watch on your set at home or on a studio monitor, try at all costs to see the interview at least once. Be really critical. Watch the replay of your interview in as detached a mood as possible and pretend you are that model viewer seeing yourself for the first time.

Did you come over as a sincere, honest person? Did you as the viewer relate to the figure on the screen? Were you in charge? Did you sell yourself? Did you sell your cause or product?

Watch the interview with your brief on your lap and tick off the key points as they come over. At least half the page should be ticked and any point scoring two ticks is good news.

There is no better critic than yourself. If you can ever sit back with a contented smile on your face, then something is seriously wrong.

CHECK-LIST

PREPARATION
Let *them* do all the fussing:
- ☐ show you to your seat
- ☐ fix microphone, etc.

(continued)

CHECK-LIST *(continued)*

Last check on clothing:
- ☐ stray hair
- ☐ straighten tie, shirt, etc
- ☐ pull down coat at back

Voice test — same volume as you'll use in the interview

APPEARANCE AND MANNER

- ☐ Sit forward in seat, leaning slightly forward.
- ☐ Use your good side, if possible.
- ☐ Look at interviewer throughout.
- ☐ Speak clearly and distinctly.
- ☐ Use your hands as much as you want, and don't be afraid of mannerisms, *but avoid:*
  - — fussy or nervous movements
  - — smoking.
- ☐ Have your notes with you if you want. Glance at them for reference, but don't read from them.
- ☐ Be *sincere* and *enthusiastic* throughout.

HANDLING THE INTERVIEW

GOLDEN RULES

1. Don't let the interviewer butt in without a fight.
2. Refute any incorrect statements.
3. Don't use jargon.
4. Stay off the defensive.
5. Remember there is only *one* viewer.
6. Don't get sidetracked.

SILVER RULES

1. Look alert.
2. Try to anticipate surprises.
3. Know when they spring something (eg a surprise film or studio guest) on you; let the viewer know.
4. Don't address the interviewer by name — remember it's the *viewer* you're talking to.
5. If the interviewer rephrases your statements, make sure he's got them right. If not, put them right at once. *(continued)*

CHECK-LIST *(continued)*

6. Avoid too many 'wells' at the beginning of your answers.
7. Don't feel you have to fill embarrassing silences. That's the interviewer's job.
8. Stay off the 'ums' and 'ers'.
9. Don't tail off with 'and so on','and so forth'.
10. Only hesitate if it's deliberate.
11. Know your facts.
12. Don't lose your temper.
13. Don't volunteer irrelevant information.
14. Watch for the interviewer getting in a harmful last word.

KEY POINTS

The *platinum* rule is to think all the time in terms of telling your own key points to the viewer, *regardless of the questions and other distractions*.

Practise ways of getting points over:
- [ ] think of something you want to say
- [ ] think up a nasty question
- [ ] put the two together!

COMPLAINTS

- [ ] As a general rule don't cry over spilt milk.
- [ ] But if they overstep all bounds of decency be ruthless; hit them with everything until the record is put straight.
- [ ] Take a tape-recorder into a recorded interview, and tape the final result for comparison.

SELF-ASSESSMENT

- [ ] Watch the result as objectively as you can and see how you've measured up against this chapter.
- [ ] Check off the points on your brief to see how many you got over.

7. Different interviews - and how to handle them

Types of programme

Television has dozens of different programmes. There are old movies, serials, series, children's programmes, cabaret and a host of others.

Most of these are for the professionals — actors, presenters, singers, comedians — which leaves just three types of programme for 'outsiders' to have a chance of communicating with the viewer.

1. News

(a) MAIN NEWS
At certain times of day a TV channel tells you what's been happening via newscasters, film, correspondents and interviews.

The advantage for you of getting on the main news is that the audience is very large. Of course you still act as if there's only one viewer, but if you're promoting a campaign or company you can get through to tens of millions of people in one go. That's about the only advantage, though.

One disadvantage is that news items are brief — on average about two minutes each. By the time the newscaster has said his bit and they've shown some film, your slot can be anything from a minute down to five seconds, which means only one key point. They might have spent half the day filming you at your home but you'll be lucky if more than half a dozen sentences come over on the news programme.

Incidentally, don't be too put out when you get to the end of a perfectly good filmed interview and the producer says 'Right, now let's do it again with a bit more emphasis on . . .' Some producers are more perfectionistic (or neurotic) about it than others, but it's a common occurrence, and you may as well go along with it for a while — especially if it gives you a chance to make your own performance even punchier.

If you think they're doing too many of these takes, then you can simply tell them you've had enough and your co-operation has come to an end. However, there is seldom any demand for more than two or three.

It's not like making commercials, where some poor devil spends all day puffing at hundreds of cigarettes, trying to look cool and sophisticated when in fact he's fighting not to throw up. Or the true tale from a low-budget spaghetti western being made in the middle of Italy where, on the fiftieth take of the blonde heroine being rescued from the baddies, she was heard to say: 'Goddam, I knew who to screw to get into this film but who do I screw to get out of it!'

Another disadvantage of main news is that it's mostly bad news. Never mind *why* it's bad news. Every newspaper, commission of inquiry, psychiatrist, sociologist, PR man and TV expert has flogged this question to death. All we're interested in for the purpose of succeeding on the box is the fact that most items in a news summary are about fires, murders, kidnaps, hijacks, strikes, plagues, droughts, crashes, financial collapses and the English soccer results. So for whatever reason you appear on a news programme, it's more important than ever to plug your *good news* angle.

(b) DIARY
Then there's the 'diary' type of news. This is usually broadcast early in the evening, with anything up to an hour of 'round and about' material covering mainly local information.

Here they're more likely to be interested in your new factory or the fact that you've started a Society for the Abolition of Mothers-in-Law. Interviews are longer, there's more background information and the news doesn't have to be bad so long as it's interesting. The interviews are also generally less aggressive.

2. Documentary
This really means any kind of programme dealing with facts. Some are dramatized, but you are only interested in programmes which will involve films of interviews about *you*. Maybe the whole programme will be about you, though

you're more likely to feature as a part only.

For our purposes we can regard documentaries as divided into two broad categories:

(a) INVESTIGATIVE
'Investigative' is a television euphemism for setting out to prove something, and investigative programmes want careful handling if you're involved. Be especially wary of anything that's filmed.

They will cheerfully visit your premises for a week and film everything that moves, smiling all the while and helping you drain your best brandy. They will interview you in the mildest possible manner and you will all part the best of friends. This, more than any other time, is when you should insist on seeing any film in its final form because the end result may well knock you to pieces.

Go for a live interview whenever possible. If they insist on film or nothing, then you're faced with one of the toughest personal decisions in television communications. If you refuse to help, you stand a strong chance of being damned in your absence. ('Professor Smith claims that battery-produced eggs are poisonous. Mr Will E Makit of Basket Eggs refused to comment.')

If, on the other hand, you co-operate, there is the danger of their using selected items from your film to prove their point.

Only you can decide this one in the light of the facts at the time. On balance it's still best to think positively in terms of doing the programme. If so, latch on to the producer from start to finish. Tell him the real picture, probe him on his own views and make it perfectly clear that if he messes you around you will personally make his life hell.

(b) DESCRIPTIVE
The television people will howl with indignation and claim that there's no difference, that all documentaries are descriptive and that all investigative programmes are unbiased.

But for us on the other side of the camera, there's a big difference. Look for it when watching television. A 'descriptive' programme shows how something is made, explains new developments, describes an organization.

The descriptive documentary would show all aspects of Makit's plant for the edification of the viewer. The investigative documentary would end up proving that eggs are bad for you, or that Makit was into the company for half a million. A descriptive documentary is the nearest you can get to a straight free advert. It should be handled positively, responsibly and given all the help you can.

So how do you tell the difference? It's not possible to say here because the personnel involved in specific descriptive and investigative teams vary from year to year and country to country, and anything written now could be out of date in months.

But you can judge for yourself simply by watching. However, to confuse matters further, a few investigative teams produce responsible, unbiased programmes, while even the most responsible descriptive team will sometimes give someone the third degree.

It's up to you to assess the goodies and baddies. If still in doubt it's a case for consulting a professional television trainer or PR consultant.

3. Specialist

Specialist programmes cover a particular subject, usually weekly, and can contain any combination of material — news, documentary, film, interviews, studio interviews and panel discussions. (BBC's 'Money Programme' is a good example.)

The advantage for you on such a programme is that you're more likely to receive informed and responsible treatment. Remember, too, that these guys are often specialists in your own field, so bone up well and never bluff.

The main disadvantage is that they are the opposite to the main news in audience size. Viewers for specialist programmes are often counted in thousands rather than millions, though the people switching on to that programme may well be the group of potential customers or sympathizers you most want to influence.

Types of interview

They have ways of making you talk. The general techniques described for the straight face-to-face with one interviewer apply in all cases, but there are various types of interview, each requiring its own approach.

1. Face-to-face

This is the one we've been working on so far. You sit in a
studio and get your message over to the viewer through an
interviewer.

Sometimes there are two interviewers. This seems more
frightening than it actually is. They can't both talk at once,
so you simply act as though it's a single interviewer. Address
yourself to the one who's just asked the question.

2. Panel

It's much harder to get your points over where there's a
single interviewer, or chairman, but more than one
interviewee. No matter how many interview*ers* there are
you're still the main attraction. But with two or more
interview*ees* you have to fight for your share of the attention.

It's absolutely crucial in a panel interview for you to have
the key points from your brief thoroughly instilled into your
head, because you are going to have to hammer them out
before someone butts in and the discussion moves on to
another subject.

There will usually be a brief opportunity to get your first
main point over near the beginning when the interviewer
turns to you for a comment. With only a few interviewees
you're almost certain to be given a chance, but in those
programmes where several of you sit in the studio you may
just have to rely on jumping in at the right moment.

Panels are all about grasping opportunities. You must
judge the right moment to speak. It might be after someone
has said something that gives you a peg for what you want to
say; it may well be while someone's in the middle of speaking.
Either way, *move.*

Studio directors love to see something happening. Their
nightmare is eight screens full of impassive faces, so the
moment you want to speak, catch your director's eye (at least
one of his screens will have your mug on it) by sitting up or
forward and waving a hand or pen at the guy you want to
interrupt. *Speak immediately and keep speaking.* Most times
they will cut to you because you're providing some action.

Sometimes the chairman will shut you up for interrupting,
but at least it should put you next in line.

The only thing to watch for is that you don't make
yourself too unpopular by butting in *all* the time. Accept the

fact that you might get in only one or two points and aim to come away feeling that you got a bit more than your share without hogging all the action.

3. Straight-to-camera

Only very rarely will you get a chance to say your piece straight into the camera as though speaking to the viewer.

The advantage of the straight-to-camera interview is that the message is direct and, in the absence of questions, you have a certain amount of time to put over your message.

The disadvantage is that the politicians have ruined its credibility. It should be almost perfect to have your image projected right into the sitting-room, talking eyeball-to-eyeball with the viewer. Unfortunately so many hucksters have poured their propaganda out by this means that the viewer tends not to believe anything said straight-to-camera except by a recognized presenter.

Don't despair. This type of interview is not likely to occur, and if it does there are three golden rules:

(a) Pretend the camera is your model viewer.
(b) Picture it as your spouse or your cousin Mabel and give it an honest, earnest and sincere pep talk. Look it in the lens, only glancing at your notes if it's absolutely essential.
(c) Know *exactly* what you want to say. It destroys your image if you suddenly break off, umming and erring, to read through your notes or search for the right expression. Practise your spiel beforehand sitting on a chair and looking into a doorknob or alarm clock (making sure that you've put the cat out and your staff or relations have been forewarned!).

The usual points are still valid. Sit forward in your seat. Don't be afraid of gestures or mannerisms. In the unlikely event of being offered 'autocue' — the roll of script just above or to one side of the camera, used by newsreaders — treat it with respect. It's a great little device for the practised performer, but unless you're good with it you can easily give a dull performance.

4. Down-the-line

This type of interview is becoming increasingly popular,

which is a pity because it's a second-class way of appearing on television.

It occurs when you are in place A and the programme is being produced in place B, so they sit you down in front of the camera in A and relay your picture to a screen in the studio at B, where the interviewer is situated. (Are you still with me?) Your face appears on a screen there and you receive the questions by remote control 'down the line'.

You see the interviewer on a studio monitor. The best bet here is to ask for the monitor to be placed roughly where you would expect the interviewer to be sitting. You then address the interviewer through the monitor as in a normal face-to-face interview.

It's a lonely and unreal situation. You feel self-conscious and even the most experienced performers look a little lost when their faces appear on the screen for the first time. You just have to be as natural as you can and pretend that the camera is your cousin Mabel and that the remote voice is coming from an interviewer who is sitting beside you.

Otherwise all the old techniques apply — looking alert, gestures, key points, sidetracks and so on.

5. Telephone

More common on radio than television, but on certain types of programme, when they want to talk in a hurry to a lot of different people, including you, they will sometimes interview you on the phone. If the interview is pre-arranged they will sometimes flash a photograph of you — possibly holding a telephone receiver — with a credit showing who you are.

The 'phone-in' technique is dealt with later in the section on radio. The main thing to remember is that the telephone plays hell with your voice and you need to speak twice as clearly as you do normally.

6. Outside programmes

Outside programmes cover the same types of interview that we've already discussed but take place away from the studio.

They are more often filmed than live for the simple reason that outside transmission requires a truckload of sophisticated equipment and costs several times more than a film unit. Also, a small army of technicians is required for an outside broadcast team.

There can be few walks of life where so many hands have so little to do, so television companies like to send a small film crew.

A popular story among TV people is that of the Ten Commandments: Moses comes down from the mountain to find dozens of camera crews waiting for him. There are NBC and BBC, ITN, ZDF and all the other big stations. They grill Moses in depth on his findings and depart. That evening in every country a newscaster comes on the screen for the main news: 'Good evening. Today Moses returned from his ascent of Mount Sinai with ten commandments. Here are the main three . . .'

Doing an interview away from the studio has its advantages and you should be able to create a slightly better impression than in the studios. It's partly because you are more confident on your own territory and partly because the viewer's attention is more attracted; it's a different scene from the boring old studio.

For our purpose, outside interviews fall into three categories:

(a) OUT OF DOORS

People tend to treat a television interview like sexual intercourse and assume that it must be conducted in a room with no windows and a locked door.

Nothing could be further from the truth. An alfresco interview takes a lot of beating. Of course, you often see people interviewed at their factory gates (or in front of its smoking remains), but why not in any case suggest to the producer that you meet in the park or in your garden?

Assuming the weather's OK, you'll feel infinitely more relaxed and in control, and the setting will be a pleasing change for the viewer.

As with all things, there's a disadvantage. In this case it's distractions. You can be half-way through a brilliant, dynamic attack on the allocation of social security payments, when some kid with an ice cream comes along and stands behind you, waving at the camera. Or a multi-engined jet liner flies 30 feet over your head.

Watch out, too, for your personal appearance out of doors, such as the wind ruffling your hair. (Also watch out for passing pigeons!) But, generally speaking, outdoor interviews are good news.

(b) INDOORS

The next best thing is an interview at your own desk or in your home. You hold the territorial advantage and will tend to be more confident. Don't be tempted to relax too much by sinking back into your favourite settee or spinning round in your executive chair. It's still vital to look alert and be alert.

A small point, which applies to radio interviews too: avoid large or unfurnished spaces. Your voice echoes in such locations.

Again, watch out for interruptions. Take the phone off the hook and if possible get someone to stand outside the door to stop people bursting in or practising the drums in the playroom.

(c) DOORSTEPPING

This is where you're emerging in an advanced state of weariness from day-long strike negotiations, and some clown sticks a microphone under your nose.

The 'doorstep' interview, where they catch you coming out of the building, is supposed to give a story urgency and atmosphere. Here's the man-in-the-know coming straight from the meeting and the viewer gets the latest dope right from the horse's mouth. Actually it's baloney, because if you analyse it you'll see that people on doorsteps are much less informative than they are in the studio, but at least it gives the viewer a bit more excitement to see politicians or strike leaders backed up against a door by dozens of cameras, like the St Valentine's Day massacre.

In all fairness, it's usually done in a crisis where several TV network teams want to talk to the same person all at once and in a hurry.

Or there's the 'man-in-the-street' interview, which is done to give the impression of an on-the-spot survey. There's something in this as people do tend to give their immediate reaction.

Don't worry too much about being stopped in the street. The odds are 100:1 on that you'll be asked your views on the new bypass or something like that. Even then you might be quick off the mark and give your own favourite subject a plug.

The doorstep situation is more serious. If you refuse to speak you can be sure they'll soon find someone else — probably on the other side — who *will* speak.

This is the time to make one quick point and call it a day. If you can actually answer their question, so much the better, but it's more likely that you'll be asked something tricky. Let's look at some examples of how to use the questions on the spur of the moment:

- ☐ 'Mr Adams, how are the strike negotiations progressing?'
- ☐ 'They're not over yet, but let me assure you that the customer will be eating our bread again as soon as possible.'
- ☐ 'Miss Makepeace, how do you feel about being found guilty of obstructing the highway?'
- ☐ 'I'd do it again if it stopped them building that nuclear power station. One accident at one of those places and we'll all be dead.'

If the doorstep interview continues, carry on with the same formula as long as you're happy you can handle it. Then walk off. It requires quick thinking to assess what you want to get over, but then the principles are the same as for a full-scale studio interview.

Don't get drawn into blurting out an answer to a question that you really shouldn't answer on the spot.

- ☐ 'Is it true that your marriage has broken up?'
- ☐ 'I'll make a statement in due course. This isn't the time'

is about all you can do. Always stay calm and courteous.

Remember: Different programmes want handling in different ways, but the basic principles are always the same.

CHECK-LIST

TYPES OF PROGRAMME

There are 3 main types of programme for our purposes:

1. News

   (a) Main news
   ☐ advantage: big audience.
   ☐ disadvantages: very brief items, generally bad news.
   (b) Diary
   ☐ general interest: longer items, usually good news.

2. Documentary

   (a) Investigative
   ☐ out to prove something, often unfavourable.

   (b) Descriptive
   ☐ informative, positive.

3. Specialist

   ☐ deals regularly with a particular subject.
   ☐ advantage: informed and responsible.
   ☐ disadvantages: small audience.

TYPES OF INTERVIEW

1. Face-to-face

   You and the interviewer(s) facing each other in the studio.

2. Panel

   2 or more interviewees. You may have to fight for your share of the action. Choose your moment to speak, then *move.*

3. Straight-to-camera

   ☐ advantages: direct message, more time.
   ☐ disadvantage: credibility gap.

CHECK-LIST *(continued)*

Remember 2 rules:
- ☐ Pretend the camera is your model viewer.
- ☐ Know exactly what you want to say.

4. Down-the-line

    Remote control interview with you in another studio. Treat camera as the viewer, and the monitor as the interviewer.

5. Telephone

    See radio section.

6. Outside programmes

    (a) Out of doors
    - ☐ good, try it for a change.
    - ☐ more relaxed, and more attention from the viewer.
    - ☐ but beware of distractions.

    (b) Indoors
    - ☐ office or home — you have territorial advantage, but don't relax too much.
    - ☐ avoid empty room and distractions.

    (c) Doorstepping
    - ☐ where you're ambushed by camera crews.
    - ☐ remember to get *your* case over by using the questions.
    - ☐ if you really can't answer, don't.

8. Television training courses

The idea of training people to do better on television is relatively new. Though some training courses have been in action for ten years or more, each newcomer to the scene still gets treated by the press as a wonderful new concept. This is no bad thing as a good training course can be of immense benefit.

The biggest single advantage is that of actually seeing yourself on the screen, for the only way you can possibly know how you appear to others is to be filmed in action.

The effect can be horrifying. For the first time people see their personal tics — blinking, nervous smiles, irritating mannerisms, shifty eyes. They can judge for themselves whether or not they come over as sincere, earnest types, or whether they seem pompous, flippant, neurotic or downright shady.

If you are ever likely to have to appear on television (and presumably if you've got this far into the book then you *are* likely to), a training course should go straight to the top of your priorities list.

Types of course

Seeing yourself on the box is the main advantage but there are many others, depending on the quality of the course. It's valuable to practise being interviewed, for one thing, and useful to get the 'feel' of a studio for another.

Television training courses are a strange mixture. Each seems different in its approach, yet at the end of the day the effect on the student is pretty much the same. Some go for plugging a few simple rules, others spend days covering all aspects of television and radio.

Most people running these courses are poachers-turned-gamekeepers. After a few years producing programmes and interviewing they start to work for themselves and teach others how to survive in the studio. For some, George Bernard Shaw's maxim: 'those who can, do; those who can't, teach' applies. Others are cashing in on their television success, or even moonlighting — grilling interviewees one day and the next day teaching them how to fight back.

Quite a few of the larger courses use hired guns. They will pay a television name to come in for half a day to give the students a workout. This helps to familiarize you with the real thing (and helps the organizers to sell places on their course), but the advantages are dubious. The television pros tend inevitably to be sympathetic to their own cause, and are not necessarily better at instructing than an experienced trainer.

Value for money varies amazingly. The range is from less than £100 for two days, to over £1000 for a small group for one day (with one de luxe course in New York parting its clients from $10,000) and cost is certainly no criterion for quality. Facilities vary a fair bit too. Some trainers have just a small black and white camera, one microphone and videocassette recorder, while for the same money you can spend two days in the massive, broadcast-quality studios run by the Church of England — originally set up to train 'television vicars' but now also used for businessmen, politicians and anyone else who wants to learn studio survival.

There are 'soft' courses and 'hard' courses. Some are as dogmatic about the single path to righteousness as the Spanish Inquisition; others leave you confused and having to work out too much for yourself. Some operate in a particular geographical region, some are centred in the capital, while still others follow their clients around.

Having established the need to try a training course — if only to know what you look like on television and to get some interview practice — the next thing is to work out the maximum amount of time and money you can afford.

It's like learning to fly an aeroplane. First you have to learn to fly; then you have to stay in practice. It's a hard enough technique in the first place, and quite expensive, but it doesn't end there. After a good training session you may be ready for anything but it doesn't take long to get out of

practice. The cost of a couple of training courses a year is but
a small insurance to avoid crash landings.

Group or solo?
Because we hate making fools of ourselves, many people —
especially top businessmen — prefer personal grooming.

Of course, private treatment is feasible and most trainers
will give it at a price. A full TV training session is a lot to
absorb in one go, however, and it's often best to spread it
out a bit. The exception is when you want a quick training
session to practise a specific interview immediately before
going to the studios.

A group of three to five (six is an absolute maximum)
people can watch each other's performances and
constructively criticize them, learning about themselves in
the process. They can also 'switch off' between interviews —
which just isn't possible on your own — and it's cheaper.

Which course?

Choosing the right training course can be difficult. There's no
association to refer to, no adverts, no 'good training guides',
though there are an increasing number of satisfied or
dissatisfied clients for word-of-mouth recommendation.

However, there are two effective ways of picking a good
course:

1. Pick a winner
It's like finding out there's no Santa Claus. The terrible truth
is that most successful performers go in for some form of
training. A few are 'naturals', but the majority of politicians,
campaigners and union leaders who appear regularly and
successfully on the small screen are highly trained.

So one way to latch on to an effective course is to watch
television, watch interviews, watch for the winners and make
a note of who they are. Then look up their PR people and ask
them who does their TV training. This applies more in the
case of successful business spokesmen than, say, politicians
who are often natural pros.

It won't be as simple as it sounds. Some of them won't
have a PR office, some won't admit to having been trained,
some won't have been trained anyway. But the chances are

that if you look up, say, five good television spokesmen, ask for their PR managers and say that you want advice on TV training, at least one of them will put you on to a good training course.

There's no need to be furtive about it. Simply say who you are and why you're asking.

2. Bet on the field
Having established that one course alone isn't enough, there's a lot to be said for trying a number of different courses anyway. This way you'll pick up all the tips and techniques that different people have to offer and will soon know the good from the bad. Once you find one you really like you can stick to it.

Course programme

Training techniques — and the people behind them — differ, but courses follow a broadly similar pattern. A typical programme over, say, one day, might be:

1. Introductory talk
Self-explanatory. Often you'll be told 'It's all very friendly. We're here to enjoy ourselves.' This may be true of the course in general, but don't believe a word of it when the interviewing starts. It's like the dentist saying 'This won't hurt a bit.'

2. Straight-to-camera
Many courses make their first exercise a two-minute straight-to-camera talk. Having been told in the introductory talk about making your main points, you take it in turns to go into the studio and give it a whirl.

Presumably this is to break the ice, though it always strikes me as a relatively useless exercise. It's all right in a thorough training programme where there is time to do some straight-to-camera work, but the real-life chances of ever having to do a straight-to-camera item are so remote that the time would be better spent doing double the interview practice.

However, it's regarded as a good thing by some pundits and is certainly an education if it's the first time you've seen yourself as others see you. For most people the time flashes by and the cameraman is giving the 'wind-up' signal before you're half-way through saying what you wanted to say.

The popular choice is to speak about your company or calling. That's not a bad way to practise working to a brief with only two or three key points, but for a change from all the serious stuff, why not talk about your favourite sport or hobby? Or try a descriptive piece, like describing a football game or historic building, and get some practice at 'painting a picture' for the viewer?

Each session is then followed by a playback and critique. These are useful as a means of learning to look for faults and good points in others, as well as finding out about your own technique.

3. Film

At some stage there may be a session in which the students see film or videotape of how it should and shouldn't be done. This shows interviews etc with past students and, sometimes, actual television programmes.

4. Studio interview

This is the crunch. At last you get the feel of coming under fire and have a chance to practise your interview technique. It's quite common to feel terrified the first time, but you'll probably notice how little the nervousness actually shows on the playback.

Some courses work hard to get plenty of interviews in, which is to their credit. You should still feel tense prior to *every* interview, but by the second and third times it's that much easier, and you'll see some improvement on the playback. Unfortunately quite a few courses are guilty of devoting too much time to chat, lunch and peripheral stuff like straight-to-camera techniques, so that by the end of the day you've only done one interview.

Another criticism of almost all courses is that they omit to give you a 'soft' interview. Certainly, a ruthless grilling is the most essential part to practise, but it's almost as important to learn to handle an easy one.

After all, the majority of interviews on television — especially local programmes — are fairly friendly affairs. Now, if all your training has been devoted to withstanding a barrage of loaded questions, you can find yourself out of your depth if the interview consists of just one or two general and perfectly answerable questions. It can be harder to appear alert, lively and sincere in front of a friendly interviewer than a hostile one. There's also a temptation to talk too much when the questions aren't being slammed in every 20 seconds.

5. Down-the-line

The technique of sitting on your own, answering a remote voice, is generally only practised in longer courses of two days or more, simply because it's impossible to cram everything into a single day. It's a pity, because although the interview principles are the same as for face-to-face, a down-the-line interview has a different atmosphere. It's disconcerting not to be able to talk directly with your tormentor, and a bit of practice can be very useful.

6. Panel

This is often the final session involving all the students together. It's important training, because items with two or more interviewees are popular, and the chances are quite high that you will have to hold your own in a group.

One last tip: in your encounters with television trainers look for one or two good ones who are in the market for giving clients a last-minute brushing-up session before going on the air. Nothing can beat going into the studio having just spent an hour practising interviews on that particular topic with an expert trainer. It will be worth every penny.

Television training – a TV man hits back

Nobody hates television training more than the people in television. Just as a lot of interviewees have bad experiences when interviewed, so a lot of programme-makers suffer from interviewing people who walk into the studios like computerized robots, intoning their 'three key points' and attacking from the bell.

The following example is ridiculous but true: a town council recently came under fire for procuring a luxury mansion and renting it out to council house tenants. The council's chairman, ready for a punch-up, sat in the studio all but fingering his knuckledusters while a brief film was shown about the mansion and the plans.

Then he was introduced by the interviewer, who led in with a perfectly reasonable and predictable question: 'Mr X, why has your council bought this house?'

But our friend had done his training, hadn't he? Quick as a flash he laid into the interviewer: 'Ah, this is one of your trick questions. I'm not going to answer it!'

Goodbye Councillor.

All the 'tough' training, both in this book and on many television training courses, is done in the simple belief that the interviewee will have the common sense to know when to fight and when not to.

This is just one of the reasons why business and television are so often at loggerheads. Both sides keep quoting the extreme examples.

I invited John Swinfield, the editor of Anglia Television's lively and responsible business programme, 'Enterprise', to put the TV man's case *against* television training.

As expected, he pulls no punches, yet much of what he says is in no way inimical to this chapter. There is plenty of good advice: for example, the tips about mannerisms.

The real answer to success lies between the two. If you go on a television course that indoctrinates you in a fixed routine, then quickly read the following as an antidote. But remember, too, that the people inside television are great at telling you to jump in without a life-jacket.

'I think some rum things are being said in this tome about me and mine in television. One gets the impression we are all out to get you — below the belt — in public. That is not true.

'Most people in television, like most anywhere else, cry into their beer and enjoy sleeping at night with relatively easy consciences. It is preposterous conceit to suggest that all television people are twisting, heartless charlatans. A handful might be. Most are not. It is as silly as saying all businessmen are on a par with Nixon and his plumbers — or are all as pure as driven snow.

'But perpetrating myths has always been a good money maker. The more you tell businessmen that inside every programme maker there is an unsmiling Leninist, or a rapscallion enticing you into a devil's polka where you don't know what you're saying or why you're saying it, then — presumably — you will sell more primers like this.

'Terrified men of commerce, or whatever, will hand over outrageous amounts of money, no doubt written off to expenses, believing it to be cheap at the price if they are to be steered safely around the bloody cleavers wielded by this band of pitiless media butchers.

'The fashionable ploy, and it is a most lucrative trade, is to direct you to some television training course where stuffed have-beens are employed as interrogators-in-residence. They are supposed to act like leading interviewers — putting unfortunates through a grilling routine rarely encountered outside Fleming escapism.

'A dingy basement, or a swanky thick pile routine, with toy equipment, is supposed to be a replica of a real studio.

'I know about such goings-on because I have succumbed in the past to the lure of pound notes — thrust at me by pin-striped, pink gin PR men — wanting me to make their sometimes eminent clients grovel and squeal under the lights. Then, having stripped them of what little confidence they had in the first place, they can then rebuild them, at a price, with a whole new television personality, tailor-made, glossy and plausible.

'In my own defence I must add that I have usually told the poor blighters who are being "trained", like mannered seals in a PR circus, that I do not believe I could do much for them. Rather than take their money I have always made it clear that I would quite understand if they wanted to make a dash for it. Once, one of the learners — the head of an enormous corporation — actually heeded me, fumed at his public relations man who had lured him there, shook my hand, and left. The PR man then refused to pay my fee — even suggested I owed him money having lost him a client — and it nearly ended in fisticuffs rolling around the floor of that fake studio.

'You can believe this, or believe it not, but if you are as honest as possible — both before and during your appearance on television — then you really should have little to fear from most programme makers and interviewers. If you feel you can only appear by telling untruths, or half the truth, then you should stay clear. If your motivation is simply to gain kudos for yourself, or your company, or whatever else it might be, while boring the pants off an audience, you should also stay away.

'Try and give your television hosts a full and accurate picture of yourself — and whatever it is you have been invited in to chunter on about — not so that he or she can catch you out, but so that they can be diplomatic. You cannot expect an interviewer to respect confidences if you do not tell him what they are — and it can happen quite easily that an interviewer will stray, unwittingly, into an area that could cause you intense embarrassment.

'Of course, every trade has bad apples, and you will just have to take a risk on that. That is being brutally honest and there is damn all you, or your public relations man, can do about it. But, in the main, members of my craft live in a world of confidences —

and if they are any good, they usually respect those confidences and do not break them. Journalistic careers are not built on confrontations where the interviewer has cheated.

'It sounds crass, but try and be yourself. Do not worry about the odd cough or splutter, or the fact that you perhaps cannot find exactly the right word at the right time. Such trivialities are perfectly human and natural. Obviously it is better not to pick your nose, go rabbitting on, or fiddle nervously with your keys, flies, or clammy notes that went down a treat at last year's cricket club dinner but are no good at all in a live interview.

'Try and trust implicitly in the television people around you — they are all professionals — and they are there to help you. The interviewer wants a good, honest, and lively story. If you are evasive he will, and should, pursue you. If that is going to be the case — I have little sympathy for you. You should not have gone there, you were a silly chump, and you should not have been vain enough to think that you could flannel your way through with some total or partial fabrication.

'If you think something is an unfair question — or one that betrays a confidence — say so. But try and say so with grace — a smile, a twinkle in the eye, goes a long way. Do not try and put the interviewer down. He is better than you at that sort of game.

'Always remember, and this should be a great confidence booster, that no matter how well a programme or an interviewer has done his research, you will always know more about yourself and your business than they can ever know. So you should always have the edge. If you can make important business decisions, involving sometimes great amounts of money, with far reaching consequences, then surely there is nothing to be frightened about in the sort of five-minute chat that constitutes 90 per cent of television in this country.

'Having given up television "training" on grounds of principle, I should really turn down a fee for contributing to this book — which, as I have said, I am convinced is all part of a burgeoning public relations spoof.

'But having given you some of the soundest — and most truthful — advice in the entire volume, I cannot see one good reason why I should not be paid for it.'

OK, so he doesn't like it! Be your own judge. Watch a few interviews and decide for yourself if you want to go in cold.

9. Do-it-yourself training

With a set in most homes, television presents plenty of opportunities for self-training. Having taken in the techniques, you can see them at work in real-life interviews and assess the cases where the techniques could have been applied.

It doesn't take long to recognize the experts and those with a natural gift. Before long, too, you'll be groaning inwardly as some unconscionable bore drones away or a hapless victim withers beneath a verbal knife-throwing act.

By watching television in that frame of mind the techniques become second nature. It's possible to develop a sense for the loaded question, a knack for turning answers into key points and the ability to side-step the heavy tackles.

Quite a few people are able to take it a stage further and get in some 'dry' training. Businessmen with PR staff or advisers, heads of organizations — in fact anyone who can coerce someone else into acting as interviewer — can sit down somewhere quiet and run through some practice questions. It's not as good as seeing yourself on the screen but it's useful all the same.

Build your own studio

But nothing can beat having your own studio, and it's cheaper than you think. It's easy to spend literally millions on equipment, as some organizations do, but in fact an adequate training studio can be established for the cost of a month's salary of an average chief executive. At that price it seems ridiculous that only a handful of companies have their own TV studios.

The requirements are simple:

1. Room
About 150 square feet is ample space. It can be less if
necessary. Go for a high ceiling and light walls if possible. The
quieter the better, and there must be a means of blocking out
the light. It's essential to have some form of ventilation as it
gets mighty hot in there. The furnishings can be sparse. You'll
want a couple of chairs, preferably low armchairs that swivel.
A table is needed for the TV set and another for the
recording equipment (or one large table will do).

2. Television set
If you're skimping, a second-hand black and white job is all
that's needed. However, a colour set is preferable for two
reasons:

(a) Your recording equipment will be able to receive and
    record TV programmes in colour. As you'll be using it to
    record your own real television interviews (and any other
    programmes you want) it's nicer to be able to play them
    back in colour — for which a colour set is necessary.
(b) The units in our simple studio can be built up, so if you
    eventually graduate to colour cameras you'll already
    have the set.

3. Camera
A simple, electronic, black and white camera costs just a
few hundred pounds. It has to be electronic to transmit the
signal to the recording equipment. One luxury that really *is*
worthwhile is a zoom lens. It adds plenty of realism.

   You'll want a tripod for the camera with a swivel top to
pan from interviewer to interviewee and back.

4. Videocassette recorder (VCR)
In their infinite wisdom, the manufacturers of video recorders
have created two different types of equipment, each
requiring a different size of cassette. The two are
incompatible, and exponents of each system will talk
themselves blue in the face arguing which is best.

   The experts argue that the Sony type is best because you
can produce broadcast-quality tapes (if you're prepared to
spend a few grand on broadcast-quality cameras) and the
equipment is supposed to be more reliable. On the other hand,

it's more expensive, and the portable models are even more expensive.

The Philips system comes cheaper and even the cheapest models are relatively portable.

You get what you pay for. The experts are supposed to be right, but as part of the exercise is to save money, check with your dealer to get the best value without spending a fortune.

VCRs are becoming increasingly popular as household toys for recording television programmes, and a lot of fun they are too. You can watch your favourite goal again and again or, better still, pre-set the machine to record your favourite series while out at a boring cocktail party. It's even possible to record one channel silently while watching another on the same set, so we could well see a drop in the divorce rate as sales of VCRs increase!

But few people realize that the same equipment takes a signal from your own camera with little or no modification, depending on compatibility between the camera and VCR. Thus the image from the camera and sound from the microphone are recorded electronically on the cassette tape and can be played back as quickly and as often as you like.

4. Microphone
One decent mike standing on the small table, between you and the 'interviewer' and to one side, will suffice for a start. To some extent it restricts movement, because you lose the sound if you turn your head away, but it's no great problem.

5. Lights
Good lighting is, of course, necessary to get a picture, and in addition a couple of powerful lamps make all the difference to the realism.

Until the lamps are switched on you know that you're simply sitting in a small room with some mickey mouse equipment doing a mock interview. But switch on two or three strategically placed one-kilowatt theatre lights (on stands, of course) and it instantly becomes as close to the real thing as you can get. The lights are hot and bright and you can hardly see beyond the interviewer and the camera lens.

So much for the basic equipment. The outfit described

can cost less than a cheap car and is adequate for the job.
According to available funds you can then build up. The first
improvement to go for is a second camera for added realism,
followed by clip-on microphones. The well-to-do can go to
colour cameras and broadcast-quality recording equipment,
though it won't make you perform any better.

Meanwhile two other important items of equipment are
essential:

6. Camera operator
Another good argument for keeping the camera(s) cheap and
simple is that an elementary black and white camera can be
operated efficiently by any secretary, wife or neighbour with
only a few minutes' tuition. Elaborate colour jobs need
elaborate operators.

7. Interviewer
This is much more of a problem. You can't interview yourself,
and an inexperienced interviewer will do more harm than
good. Businessmen with PR people can send someone off on
a TV training course, but those with smaller outfits will
simply have to scout around for someone to do the job for
them — maybe a local journalist or interviewer from a local
radio station. They are notoriously underpaid and may well
do the job for a small backhander.

Unfortunately it's not an easy market. Television
interviewing is an art of its own and you are going to have to
find a gifted amateur from somewhere. It can be done.

Once you've got your own studio the sky's the limit. You
and your colleagues can improve all the time and you will
have the inestimable benefit of being able to brush up shortly
before going to the studios. It might even be possible to
persuade other companies to rent your studio when you're
not using it.

(A last word of warning: a newly-wed couple in Turin
recently treated themselves to VCR equipment and put it to
the unusual use of recording their love-making for extra kicks.
By a million-to-one chance, unfortunately, the recording
equipment was faulty and 'broadcast' the entire proceedings
to all the other television sets in the apartment block!)

10. Television's treatment of business

If you're getting a bit punch-drunk about television by now, here's some good news.

We've been looking at the tough side of television — the atmosphere in the studio, the angles and tricky questions, the antipathy towards business.

But it's by no means all bad. The muck-rakers are fortunately in the minority and most programmes, while not necessarily making life easy, try to be as fair and unbiased as they can. That doesn't mean you can relax. If you go into every interview equipped for a fight you'll both survive the hard ones and put on a much better showing in the easy ones.

The really great news, though, is that the future looks increasingly brighter for business. Television has been through some black years, especially in America, when trashy entertainment and advertising were the only programmes the demi-gods of broadcasting would sanction.

Then some programmes started to appear with more serious, informative content. Science was found to be interesting and economics acceptable, and now even business is starting to creep in at the edges.

Unequivocally, British television leads the world, so it is fitting that Britain should have led the way with programmes about business. The pioneers are finding it hard going but their contribution to society cannot be overstated. In this chapter we'll look at the work of two people — Michael Blakstad and John Swinfield — who are relative unknowns, yet who are doing more than any trade union or corporation to get the man in the street to realize the importance of business to our existence.

The United States

Let's look first at the States, where business still comes under the general heading of 'current affairs', but where at least current affairs, which include commerce and industry, are increasing in stature at an incredible rate.

News was once a sort of mandatory 'filter' between the old films and commercials, but by 1974 surveys showed that the average time spent by viewers watching news and public affairs had risen to a remarkable 25 per cent, and the indications are that the figure is still rising.

News has become big news. Reporters like Geraldo Rivera at WABC-TV, New York, and Marvin Zindler at Kirk-TV, Houston, have become prominent figures in their quest for the truth. A few years ago WABC's idea of a two-hour programme on consumer affairs, local government, etc, would have been written off as a joke, yet now other companies are falling over themselves to copy it.

Coverage of business increases naturally with the growth in coverage of current and consumer affairs. The three major commercial networks each have a business or economics editor and there are several programmes on which businessmen appear regularly: 'Meet the Press', 'Issues and Answers', 'Face the Nation', '60 Minutes', etc.

The Public Broadcasting System has taken things a step nearer to straight business coverage with its 'Wall Street Week'. The next natural step will be for some enterprising channel to come up with its own business programme.

All the signs are that television has already accepted the world around it as important material and that the world of business will soon be getting its share of the action.

Britain

In Britain the time was never riper. Not long ago business was at the very bottom of every programme controller's list. Only a faithful few viewers huddled round their sets on a Friday night to watch 'The Money Programme', like members of the Resistance listening to an illicit wartime broadcast.

But things are changing so fast that many businessmen still don't realize it's happening.

The BBC discovered that there was excitement in new

inventions and so 'Tomorrow's World' was born, followed by 'The Risk Business' out of the same stable. Meanwhile, Granada showed the flag for the independent broadcasters with its 'Nuts and Bolts'.

Anglia, only in the middle league for size, put a daring toe in the water with its half-hourly 'Enterprise' late on a Friday night.

Within months the giant Thames Television was in there for an hour a week with its 'Time for Business', employing a hefty team of researchers and experts. (The programme was originally intended to be called 'Mind your Business', but the title was quickly shelved after a number of misunderstandings between telephone callers and employers answering the phone with 'Mind your Business'!)

Two of the pioneers of industrial coverage on television are Michael Blakstad of the BBC and John Swinfield of Anglia Television. Blakstad is editor of 'Tomorrow's World' and 'The Risk Business'. Here's his attitude to business on the box, from an article he wrote for a leading business magazine:

> 'I've listened to many pundits telling us what we ought to transmit, but none giving any convincing evidence that viewers actually want to watch programmes about industry. I am as devoted as the next man to Lord Reith's dictum that we should entertain, inform and educate, but we don't achieve any of these aims if no one is watching.

> 'Making programmes about industry is uphill all the way. Decisions are not made in the twinkling of an ulcer, amid dramatic board room conflicts (not that we'd be allowed in to film them if they were!). Events of any significance take long periods to unfold, and our budgets can't permit lingering schedules with film crews waiting for the magic moment. You company directors, whether you'll admit it or not, use a lot of words to make your points, which means that we have to edit you down. This is what worries you — but what worries me is the loud ring of the cash register as celluloid churns through the camera.

> 'Complex subjects usually require intricate graphics — another hideous cost — but no one is going to deny that industry is complex. All in all, our experience so far indicates that these are among the most expensive factual programmes in our repertoire.

> 'And there's a third obstacle. The best programmes are made by the best producers, and the best producers simply do not seem to want to work in a field where the rewards (professional, not financial) are so poor. The low prestige with which British education has endowed engineering and industry is inevitably reflected among the (slightly pampered) cultural *élite* who make

the best television programmes. Give a talented producer the choice of dealing with an important political matter for "Panorama", or pure science for "Horizon", the arts for "Omnibus" or social problems for "Man Alive" reports, and the chances are that he'll choose one of these rather than the prospect of spending long hours in drab offices or less-than-resplendent shop floors trying to squeeze blood out of the industrial stone. At least, that's the way it looks from Shepherd's Bush.

'At this point the concerned industrialist is at liberty to leap to his feet and exclaim that the main obstacle at present is television's own less-than-honourable record of industrial coverage; it's nonsense to complain that no one wants to watch when there's never been anything worth watching in the past. Perhaps these programmes will be loss leaders for a while, but the need to change the image of industry in Britain is so profound that the BBC and ITV should be encouraged to make this sacrifice; the audience will soon catch up.

'We're now back on the well-established path I have travelled with different businessmen at conferences, seminars and dinners for so many years that one could be forgiven for thinking that there really does exist a huge untapped reservoir of charismatic personalities dying to disclose their working lives to the cameras, ready to open their doors and to share with us and the Great British Public the difficult but stimulating decision points and moments of creativity which characterise both management and shop floor life in Britain. It is just that, up to now, we – the media folk – have made no concerted effort to open those doors.

'I regret to say that I can report three years of trying to take down those barricades, and a nose flattened by the number of doors that have been firmly shut in my face. Come back, we'll be told, when

(a) we've taken the decision
(b) we've negotiated it with the unions
(c) it's been proved a success
(d) you've given us written notice of your questions, so that we can submit them to the board (which will guarantee answers of stultifying dullness)
(e) our directors have been on one of those television training courses which will iron out any spark of spontaneity they possess at the moment.

'That, taken from the field, is actually quite a moderate reply. At the moment of writing there are two nationalised industries which won't talk to us at all, one on the grounds that they're doing so well that any publicity would embarrass them. A successful public company refused to co-operate "because we know our clients and we don't need television to publicise our products". The list of refusals is a long one, but I should record that the smaller concerns are, on average, much more co-operative than the large ones; this says a lot for their courage when you appreciate how much they stand to lose if their Risk Businesses turn out to be unsuccessful.

'This very British brand of non-cooperation is, in many ways, perfectly understandable. It could be enormously valuable to a competitor to see film of a new process being developed in your laboratory. Let the media in too soon, and your project may take an unexpected bad turn, and who wants to be a sacrificial lamb on the altar of 'good television'? Few managers have been asked in the past to appear on 'the box', so there is much less experience of this medium among industrialists than there is in politics, let's say, or in science. Jobs and industrial peace often depend on sensitive communication within a company, and television is not known for its kid gloves or its sensitive footwear. Television is doing fine so long as it continues the old Tomorrow's World tradition of 'positive' reporting (which is taken to mean free advertising for new products) but is to be discouraged from straying into the wilder country of in-depth reporting.

'There are, mercifully, enough sacrificial lambs willing to be offered up on the altar of better programmes to encourage us to gird our loins for a third tilt at the industrial windmill. This is the only programme area for which new jobs are at present being created and output expanded. It only remains for those who have talked long and loud about the need for these programmes to lower their defences and to make an act of faith that this kind of output does, in the long run, benefit society as a whole, even if a few have to gamble their reputations and perhaps their jobs.

'If no one comes forward, our efforts die, and it's back to the reporter outside the factory gates shouting into his microphone: "Inside, lousy management is in conflict with pig-headed unions . . ." and that is precisely what we are all trying to get away from, isn't it?'

(Extracts from an article by Michael Blakstad in *Director* Magazine, March 1978.)

Plenty of food for thought there. Note that here is another top producer who has no time for training courses. At the other end of the scale some interviewers and producers make a small fortune out of running their own courses.

Possibly the best bit of news for business on television comes from one of the smaller independent television companies. Quite recently Anglia Television decided, very daringly, to run a weekly programme on business, much of it local.

They hired John Swinfield (who wrote the attack in this book on television training) to edit and present the new programme late on Friday nights. The first series was so successful that it was moved into peak viewing time at 7.00 in the evening.

More than anyone, Swinfield has got to grips with the difficult task of presenting business as *interesting.* The programme concentrated on local industries with a story to tell, but now it wanders with equal verve into North Sea oil, consumer affairs and the business of running a national newspaper. Television profiles of leading businessmen are a regular feature.

Among the lively ideas which have lured the viewer away from old movies and pop groups are ones like the programme which took the two local soccer teams, Ipswich and Norwich, and compared their business styles. Possibly for the first time people could see that footballers are a commodity, like apples and bicycles.

On another occasion 'Enterprise' took Leslie Porter, the chairman of Tesco stores, on a surprise inspection of one of his high street stores, while one of its first exploits was its 'jobshop' — a sort of television employment agency matching unemployed people with firms looking for staff.

What was a remote slot on a remote channel now has at least one national newspaper pressing for the programme to be networked nationally.

With people like John Swinfield and Michael Blakstad proving that business is good TV material, an encouraging trend is developing in Britain. In a few years it should catch on in America.

If you are fortunate enough to make it on to one of these more responsible programmes, though, don't sit back with a sigh of relief and enjoy the ride. You'll get fair treatment, which is more than can be said for a lot of programmes, but don't forget that you're still there to sell yourself, your product, your campaign.

You don't have to go into a programme fighting. But always go in *equipped* for a fight if you have to. You are still the most important person in this whole business.

11. Bad business on the box

Nowhere does the businessman's case go by default more than on television. Business is a dirty word in most places, but when it comes to the biggest communication medium of all it's simply a joke.

Whenever businessmen and television people get together to discuss this phenomenon — which is, surprisingly, quite frequently — the discussion follows the same lines with unnerving consistency:

- ☐ 'You always show trade unionists and people knocking business. You never show our side of the coin.'
- ☐ 'That's because they're always prepared to come on the programme.'
- ☐ 'But you never ask us.'
- ☐ 'We do, but every time you say you're too busy.'
- ☐ 'That's because you always ask us at the last moment.'
- ☐ 'Television works that way. It's all last-minute stuff.'
- ☐ 'Anyway, when we do appear the questions are always loaded.'
- ☐ 'No more than we load them for the other side. We make them challenging to get an interesting debate going, but you don't know how to handle the questions.'
- ☐ 'Because we must be more cautious than the others. We've more to lose.'

And so on. It goes round in a circle and comes back to the fact that business and TV just haven't been able to mix.

Television people are creative and pushing; businessmen are usually conservative and cautious. Programme makers do things at the last minute; businessmen prefer an appointment in the diary weeks ahead. TV thrives on action and heated argument; business needs slow and calculated deliberation.

101

But there are few excuses for business being so slow to take advantage of television when other groups of people have been at it for years.

The politicians were first off the blocks. The scent of a few million potential voters attracted them like stray dogs to a bitch in season, and even in the infancy of the art, with tiny crackling silver screens set in vast walnut cabinets, the senators and MPs were pouring out the truth in its various forms.

Of the many pressure groups to take advantage of television, the trade unions have been one of the most successful. Practised at the art of standing on a soap-box from an early age, a good shop steward is a past master at communicating in short, colourful bursts. Trade unions approached television in a thoroughly professional way and went in for training courses. Add to this the fact that they have time to work at it because it's their main interest in life, and you have a formidable génre of television moguls.

The Church wasn't far behind either. Many a parishioner escapes church on a Sunday evening only to switch on the set and find himself subjected to a dose of dogma. It didn't take the clergy long to realize that they could go out into the world and preach to enormous flocks from the sanctum sanctorum of Lime Grove.

And note, too, how much more entertaining the different types of 'expert' are on television these days. Until fairly recent years, dry old subjects like science, farming and economics were as backward as business, but that's all changed. Some of television's most-loved personalities now are wildly gesticulating scientists, eccentric astronomers, entertaining economists and farmers with dung on their boots.

Stop anyone in the street and ask them to name three sportsmen, three politicians, three union leaders, etc, who they know from watching television, and to name three businessmen while they're at it. No prizes for guessing which group will get the least mentions.

Mind you, *heavy* coverage is not necessarily *good* coverage. Businessmen are quick to point out that the best-known union leaders and politicians are also the least popular because they're always in the news for causing trouble. There's some truth in this, unfortunately, which provides an excuse for staying in the office instead of facing the cameras.

However, as things are at the moment, over-exposure on television is the least of the business community's problems.

Television people give one set of reasons for the failure of business on the box, while businessmen give quite a different set. At least they all agree that there is a fundamental failing. Here are some objective reasons why:

For one thing, business is only interesting to businessmen. To everyone else it evokes images of rows of desks, dull little men in spectacles, suburban houses, forms and typewriters. It's not emotive or exciting. As the programmes mentioned in the preceding chapter show, industry and commerce are really every bit as exciting as science or farming, but people just don't see it that way — or at least they haven't in the past.

Then there is some antipathy from the studio, despite the howls of indignant protest to the contrary. So much of television is about campaigning, about social injustice, about people. So many television journalists are sociologists at heart, and virtually none of them come from a business background. It's not a deliberate bias so much as a basic lack of understanding for the role played by businessmen in life. Your belief in whether that role is good or evil will depend on your political convictions, but at least businessmen do *something*.

But the worst enemies of business are the businessmen themselves. They are appalling communicators. The key to success in politics or union affairs is the ability to communicate, but in business success is measured by how much you can keep under your hat.

While the infant politician makes a rostrum out of his play-bricks, the average businessman is actually discouraged from public appearances until he's a senior executive, by which time it's a bit late in life to start learning the nitty-gritty of communicating to hostile audiences. So they come over as incredibly dull people.

They're not really. Scratch the surface of the average director and you'll find something interesting. They have to be tough and resourceful to get where they are, and many are secretly artists, authors, inventors, free-fall parachutists and bathroom baritones. It's simply that years of caution and communicative inertia have given them a lack-lustre patina of dullness.

Underneath, their message is as vibrant and important as anyone else's, and they're desperately frustrated at not getting it over, but they simply don't know how to.

Just to make matters worse, there are one or two genuine excuses for box-shy businessmen. There are times when you just can't tell the whole truth in case it blows a contract or destroys days of delicate negotiations. While often the case, this cover is too frequently used to avoid an interview altogether.

Executives also tend to have powerful bosses, like chairmen and shareholders, who are intolerant of a word in the wrong place. This means they often have more to lose than their political and union counterparts.

They are very busy people, too, if they're successful. But more crucial than the *time* lost in appearing on television is the *distraction.* For all the other groups of TV personalities communication of their message is a major — if not *the* major — part of their job. But for a businessman the important thing is to make things and sell things, not talk about it.

As we shall see shortly, intelligent use of television can help the businessman advertise his company and achieve a favourable public opinion, but it's easy to understand how they have come to see the demands of television as a distraction from the job of making widgets.

So much for the excuses. Some are reasonable. Some are genuine but exaggerated. Some are baloney. The biggest reason for avoiding the bright lights, even if they don't admit it or even realize it, is that they're scared.

They're scared of making fools of themselves, or of upsetting someone, or of losing the argument. Businessmen are good at business, so they stick to business. They don't like unfamiliar territory one bit. There is a dearth of industrialists with the guts to have a go, and to come back fighting if it goes wrong the first time.

This leaves the field wide open to those who are willing to give it a try. At last some businessmen are waking up to the opportunities of television and starting to appear on the screen at sporadic intervals.

Quite a few big companies in Britain are going in for television training and some even have their own studios. In the US it's a major part of the business for some companies, with millions of dollars spent on in-house studio facilities.

Ford Motor, for instance, has a whole department dealing with audiovisual communications. The company's television image is given priority treatment. Spokesmen are fully briefed and made available as often as possible. The headquarters in Dearborn even has its own 'Channel Six' which collates television items important to senior executives and relays them as its own programme through closed-circuit television to some 80 sets in the building.

Still in the US, the General Electric Company has been in the audiovisual communications field for 30 years. Television systems are used to train staff in general communication techniques, and the principle of seeing themselves played back on a TV screen is excellent training for the real thing.

There is a much-needed growth among big companies in the use of video systems for in-house communications. Television can be used to each employees about developments in the company. This too requires training.

Business pressure groups are getting the message, too. The Confederation of British Industry is one of the leading lights in encouraging businessmen to get to grips with television. Here's what the Confederation's Director of Information, Dorothy Drake, has to say on the subject:

'The power of television to influence public opinion is now widely accepted by industry and commerce. Politicians and trade union officials are usually, by the very nature of their job, persuasive talkers but this is not necessarily so in the case of the businessman no matter how senior he is in his company.

'However, more and more the business community is coming to recognise that the ability to debate on television and give a polished performance is now a necessary management skill. It is also essential in the current political climate if industry's point of view is not to go by default.

'The leading employers' organisation, the Confederation of British Industry, realised this need several years ago and has since then encouraged and assisted its members and staff to become more aware of the need to be skilled television performers.

'The CBI has published its own booklet — "Don't be afraid of the box" — and has organised many television acclimatisation courses for businessmen both in London and in the provinces. This scheme has been very successful and more than 400 executives have now received training in making the most of an opportunity to appear on television.

'The courses vary in their degree of sophistication and have been held at venues ranging from full colour television studios to hotel suites. Courses usually last one day and take the participants

105

through all the likely television interviews — "face to face", "down the line", studio panel and "doorstepping" — giving advice on studio technique and information on the rights an industrialist has when participating in a programme.

'All this training is of course of no use whatsoever if those who show a flair for it do not get the opportunity to appear on television programmes. To make the best use of the talent available and to be in a position to respond to the requests from the media the CBI created a television panel.

'This panel, split into regional sections, is regularly briefed by the CBI's Press Office in London so that they are able to respond immediately to media requests.

'An example of how effective the panel can be is shown by the fact that immediately after a recent budget announcement in the House of Commons the CBI was able to field 33 spokesmen to participate in 44 separate programmes on television and radio throughout the country.

'With the number of television and radio stations growing each year and the consequent increase in available "air" and "screen" time the understanding of television and the ability to make proper use of the medium is of vital importance to industry.'

While not as developed as the CBI, other representative bodies like the Institute of Directors and the British Institute of Management go in for fielding spokesmen and running training courses. So at least we have a few pacemakers coming to terms with the facts of television life.

But there's a long, long way to go.

12. Getting a better deal

For years, television and business have eyed each other suspiciously from their opposing camps. But with the television people making a serious effort to cover industry and commerce more fully and fairly, and with a few businessmen learning the ground rules of television, things are more promising.

Businessmen are increasingly anxious for the public to understand the important role of business in the economy, in society and in day-to-day living. With some television companies making the right noises, most of the onus is now on business to get a better deal on the screen.

The immediate task is to get to grips with the principles of the chapters on 'Preparation' and 'Winning the battle' and learn to fit the basic techniques in with your own personality.

If all the businessmen — and anyone else — who appeared on television were at least able to handle the interview, to hit back on the tough questions, to know their material, to be alert and interesting, and to communicate one or two points to the viewer, everyone would benefit. The public would be more interested in business, the television programmes would be more willing to give it space, and the businessman would be invited to put his case more frequently.

Yet in a way this is putting the cart before the horse. Things will really improve when there is a fundamental change in attitudes to communication, when businessmen go on the offensive instead of just squealing 'unfair' every time they get a bad deal on television. The businessman must *want* his case to be promoted. This means a few sacrifices.

The hardest pill to swallow is that anyone entering the television arena must be prepared to lose face from time to time. The bigger the businessman, the more it hurts to be

cut down to size in public by a 24-year-old interviewer, or an
employee representative who is normally several branches
down the company tree.

The boss cats in business are accustomed to being called
'Sir', to having everyone agree sycophantically with every
utterance, to being groomed and fussed over. No way is that
going to happen inside a television studio, and the survivor
on television must accept some cut and thrust and swallow a
whole lot of pride.

Another essential is for management to receive training and
practice in public communication from an early age. This is
practised much more in America, but even there it tends to
be limited to sales and PR people.

Ideally, everyone reaching top management should have
years of experience of addressing meetings, arguing the
company case with a hostile audience, and TV interview
techniques. It's ludicrous at present that most businessmen
going on television − usually in their 40s and 50s − are
facing this sort of situation for the first time.

Most businessmen agree with the principle of more
training and experience from an early age, but balk at the
reality, and you have to sympathize with them when you see
what's involved. Any programme of this sort costs time and
money with no immediate or tangible benefit. This is
inimical to the principles of effective business.

Nevertheless, the fact remains that companies will continue
to get a raw deal on TV until they approach it with the
experience and professionalism of their union and political
counterparts.

It also means *regular* training for anyone in the firm who
is at all likely to be hauled, at short notice, out of the secure
darkness of the office and thrust into the glare of the studio
lights. Ideally it should mean in-house training with a
company studio, too. Which means even more money and,
worst of all, a time commitment by the chief executive or
equivalent.

Despite the golf and Martini image, top managers really
are very busy people and if you can get one into a mock
studio for a couple of hours you deserve a medal. But to do
it every two or three weeks . . .! Nevertheless, that's what is
needed, and it's what the other successful communicators do.

Lastly, it means being *available*, which can mean cancelled meetings, reports not written, scarce leisure time lost.

A way must be found for the businessman to see communication as one of the main functions of business, like manufacture, sales, marketing and industrial relations. And here at last is a ray of hope, because to every new proposition the good businessman will ask: 'What's in it for me?'

Well, regular and effective television coverage *does* have something to offer business. It opens a gold-mine in free advertising, as we shall now see.

13. Free advertising

The impact of television as an advertising medium is immense. Newspapers, placards, sides of buses and sandwich-men all have their place, but only with television can you push your product right into the family sitting-room.

With the TV ad you can use both sound and vision to demonstrate the indispensability of your product. You can show a captive audience how fast your cars go, how kids love eating your breakfast cereal, why beautiful women use your deodorant spray.

It's so good that there has to be a catch, and there is — money. Television advertising is expensive in the extreme.

Advertising revenues in the US, for instance, are well in excess of five billion dollars. The record was $130,000 for 30 seconds during *Gone with the Wind*, while the average for 30 seconds is $50,000.

So the business logic of spending time and effort on television training and representation is that you not only get what is effectively TV advertising for free, but you will usually actually be *paid* for it!

Putting it into perspective, you can buy your own studio equipment, send five executives on one-day courses, have ten days of private training for the top man, pay a year's salary for a television press officer and cost a month's working time for the chief executive, all for the price of *1½ minutes* of advertising on a national television programme! And that's based on UK rates which are a fraction of their American counterparts.

Of course, it's not as simple as that. An advert contains only the material you want it to. There are no hostile interviewers, no opposing participants. Besides, on an advert you show your product, not the Chairman's mug.

Against that, however, is the fact that the viewer recognizes adverts for what they are, whereas material seen and heard in a programme — especially on the news — has greater credibility.

So television interviews and documentaries score as advertising if you make sure to plug the product while remaining credible.

Success lies in ensuring that you get in a few mentions of your product and its quality. We've been over that in detail in 'Winning the battle'. At the same time, don't overdo it. People aren't fools. If you keep on reminding the viewer to eat at Joe's, he'll soon suspect something.

Use plenty of common sense. Be sensitive and sensible about how hard you plug your brand name or cause, but always go in for television programmes on the basis that you are getting some expensive advertising time for free.

And not many things are free these days.

14. Ideas for programmes

While quite a few companies do something positive about how they come over on television, a very few have taken it miles further. One or two firms have decided that if they have gone to the trouble of learning how to succeed they might as well use this new-found expertise for even more positive public relations.

It's simply an extension of the gospel we've been preaching all along: that your company – its products, location and people – can be made into news. If you're worth a two-minute interview, then why not a whole programme?

The same goes for pressure groups, politics and good causes. Television programmes love to put out material about people and what they get up to. The screen acts as a window through which the public can learn about the outside world.

The fact is that editors, producers and researchers are constantly searching for new material. Like restless armadillos they spend their lives wandering from stone to stone, turning them over in an endless search for some tasty creepy-crawlies underneath.

TV editors are frequently gaunt, haggard people who look 50 while still in their 30s. Once you see how much goes into making a programme you'll understand why.

Every minute of screen time takes hours of background work. Every programme demands a new angle on a new subject.

So they will welcome anyone who can point their noses in the direction of a new stone. Only very rarely will someone contact them and say 'I'm here!' Most of the time they have to do all their own searching, dreaming up ideas for programmes.

This is where you come in. The first job is to find out which aspects of your business will make a good programme. If you're in technology — coming up every week with some exciting new inventions — you've got it made of course, but if you produce sausage-meat or paper clips you'll need some pretty creative inspiration.

Nevertheless, most opportunities are not missed because of lack of material, but because no one thought of the television aspects in the first place.

There's the germ of a TV programme in almost any development — new products and processes, factories, environmental plans, profit-sharing schemes, marketing techniques and breakthroughs, transport methods, the food in the staff canteen and the works band.

Thousands of programmes spring from small cuttings in the newspapers which the researchers scour daily. Your chances of getting good free TV space will be much higher if you take a short cut and go direct to the programme of your choice rather than relying on them to spot a paragraph about your sale of ten tons of curry powder to India.

Put yourself in their shoes. From watching programmes yourself, think out the criteria for an interesting programme.

For a start, something has to be *original* about it. It needs to be a new development or something which is being shown for the first time. If the subject is familiar then it requires a new insight into what goes on behind the scenes.

It must be *informative*. Despite the limited intellectual level of television, people often like to feel they are being educated and increasing their knowledge of the world about them.

And above all it must be *entertaining*. The harshest enemies of responsible business presentation on television are the other channels. It only takes the flick of a switch to leave the breath-taking excitement of the moulding shop at Mickey Mouse Machine Tool Company and change to football or a good western.

So, before you pick up the phone to the television company, assure yourself that your business meets these simple criteria. If not, look for another angle which does.

Take a building company, for example. The camera crews will not come rushing to your builder's yard to film piles of brick and timber and interview you proudly expounding on your profit figures.

But it's another story if on one of your sites you're sinking piles to build houses on what was once useless swamp, or you're trying out a new building material or a new design.

Almost every company has something, somewhere, at some time, which is original and interesting enough to appeal to a television programme.

The same goes for non-business organizations. Pressure groups can get their share of the limelight, but the criteria apply just as rigidly.

The message must be original and informative and the person putting it over must command attention. This is one of the sticking points between many representative groups and television. Because they stand up for racial minorities, cripples, trade groups and business bodies, they have something worthy to say. But there's an old journalist's adage that what's *worthy* is not necessarily *newsworthy*, and nowhere is this more true than on television.

Exasperated spokesmen may spend years thinking out messages which could change the world, only to find that no one wants to listen. The onus must be on them to express themselves in such a way that people *will* want to listen.

Remember, too, that it's a continuing process. Don't simply make your mark with a TV programme once and leave it at that. Make sure they remember you're there by ringing them up every time you have something new to offer.

Having decided that you want coverage, and having then worked out what will make a good programme, the next step is to choose your target carefully. It's no good ringing up just any old programme.

Part of the formula for success on television lies in watching different programmes regularly to see who does what. Michael Blakstad, for instance, says that nothing makes him more angry than the many businessmen who complain that his programmes don't give business a fair deal, and who on being questioned show that they've never watched one of his programmes in the first place.

Some programmes are to be avoided, others welcomed with open arms. Some will go for a new product, others for a union management debate. You have to work this out for yourself by disciplined television watching in the cause of getting coverage for your business.

One thing is certain: when you pick up the phone to ring a programme you must know *who* you are phoning, and *why* you are phoning that particular programme.

Even then it will still be a pretty random process. The most seasoned PR pros can never understand why sometimes a great story gets no coverage while the next day a dead mouse under a secretary's chair will bring 20 international television crews rushing to the scene.

As with everything else in business, you just have to keep plugging away and accept the fact that maybe only one good concept in ten will actually become a television programme or part thereof.

Nor will it ever come out quite the way you envisaged it, but it is still well worth the effort. It's taking the whole thing a stage further and going to them with some positive promotion instead of waiting for them to come to you.

15. Contact with TV stations and people

Flashing a cheque-book or sending a case of Mouton Rothschild 1945 is unlikely to get you on television (at least, it *might*, but not in the way you intended!), and friends in the 'old boy' network will still only make programmes if the material is good, not out of friendship.

However, good contacts are important. You should cultivate at least one person in each of the programmes you may want to appear on. This has three advantages:

1. You can bounce your ideas off someone who always knows what the programme is looking for, and you will have some insight into their minds and way of life.
2. When you come up with an offering you are more credible than a stranger. They know you and can trust you to produce the goods.
3. While never immune from the third degree, you are less likely to be given a rough time without due warning.

This begs the questions: '*Who* should be my contacts?' and '*How* do I contact them?'

The 'how?' problem is much easier than it seems. Very few television people are as snotty as they are made out to be, and despite the glamour and remoteness of television they are really only a particular type of journalist underneath — and journalists love new contacts.

Breaking the ice should take no more than a phone call. First find the name of the person you want to contact. There are several ways of doing this, but here are three for a start:

1. Look up the name of the editor/producer, etc in the programme guide (*Radio Times* and *TV Times* in the UK, more difficult in the US where programme guides tell

you less).

2. Ring the station's switchboard and ask who the editor/
producer, etc of programme 'X' is.

3. Simply ask the switchboard to put you through to the
programme concerned. They have their own offices and
will be able to help you from there.

Once you get through to the person you want, or his
secretary, be perfectly open: 'Hello, I'm Martin Gale,
chairman of Bitchamp Industries, the riding harness people.
I'd like to tell you something about my company and
wonder if we could meet for a chat sometime.'

Think of a couple of reasons why his programme should
be interested in you, but generally there will be no problem
at all. These people are professionals and are always looking
for new leads.

Thereafter it's a question of personalities. If you hit it off
from the start then follow it up. If not, look for someone
else in the team.

Which leads to the question of 'who?', to which there is
no simple answer.

By a process of elimination you can rule out the two
extremes. Leave the chairmen and directors-general of
television companies to their own devices. No amount of
buttering them up will carry any weight with the individual
programmes. Similarly, being on drinking terms with the
janitor and messenger won't make you an overnight star.

Which leaves you somewhere in the middle, and here it's
a case of taking your pick. The editor is the key figure, but
for some purposes he may be too much of a big noise, and
a lively researcher can serve your purposes better.
Researchers are, after all, the worker ants — the creatures
who go out and do all the delving on instructions from the
editor or producer.

Editor, producer, researchers. All are important in their
ways. Ideally you should know them all. Once you've
established a good relationship with a television programme
you probably *will* know them all so the important thing now
is to start *somewhere* with *someone*.

16. Who should be spokesman?

Think long and hard about who's going to represent your company or organization on television. Some chief executives throw the onus on to a hapless minion because of 'low-key' PR (or blind funk), while others leap at the prospect of an ego trip on the silver screen. Neither is the right approach.

The important thing is to assess who best satisfies a few simple criteria.

☐ is in the know on company matters,
☐ has complete authority and discretion to speak about them,
☐ is presentable and can handle an interview,
☐ has, preferably, been trained.

The top person should be OK on points 1 and 2, but not necessarily on 3 and 4. This all sounds ridiculously obvious, but many an outfit has failed to come over on television because the wrong person was doing the interview in the first place.

If the top cat does fit the bill, so much the better. It gives an organization the maximum impact if it really is Number One doing the interview.

This can be carried further, even to the extent of having a chief who becomes a public figure. There are certain advantages in creating a figure-head for the company. The television people love it (as do the press) and if you have a chairman who comes on strong on television you will treble your coverage overnight. By being a 'character' he enhances the public standing of the company, too. Getting the sympathy of your customers — and potential customers — can be a big boost for business.

There are setbacks, though. The worst one is that there are so few business personalities around that television's appetite for them is insatiable. If he's any good there will be an unending stream of requests for him to appear, which detracts more and more from his effectiveness in running the company.

Another problem is what happens when he retires or moves on. If your public image has been built up on one key spokesman, things can go mighty flat when he leaves.

Those who benefit most from a performing figure-head are organizations such as pressure groups. Businesses at least have a tangible product or service to promote, but representative bodies, trade associations, charities and political groups are trying to sell a message or concept. This is very difficult, and many of the most successful are those where the public has related to a person more than the cause. Think of Ralph Nader and Mary Whitehouse and you begin to get the picture.

It can be an advantage to have more than one spokesman. Use Mr Big as the main one, but consider having a team of back-up people, particularly for specialist subjects, as many outfits do. If the interview is in the marketing or manufacturing areas, there's a lot to be said for putting forward a TV-trained marketing or manufacturing specialist.

The Confederation of British Industry is a good example of this. Most times the Director-General, Sir John Methven, heavily trained, comes on the screen, but the viewer is equally accustomed to seeing a good performance by the President, the Social Affairs Director *et al.*

Unfortunately public relations officers are generally unacceptable to television producers. 'We want the organ-grinder, not the monkey', is their cry. They want the 'authenticity' of a director rather than the public relations professional. The fact that the PRO may know as much about the company as the chief executive is neither here nor there. There is apparently something slick and nasty about interviewing the PR specialist, even though he represents the company in all the other walks of life.

More than one company has found a way round this by dressing up the PRO with a fancy title. A programme may well turn its nose up at interviewing the 'Press Officer' but might equally well jump over the moon at having the 'Head of Corporate Policy' or 'Executive Vice-President, Governmental Affairs' as an honoured guest. Who are they to know if it's one and the same person?

17. Radio

There were reasons for leaving radio to the end, but it's unfortunate that it had to be done. In many ways radio leaves TV standing as a communications method.

Undeniably, television is *the* medium for transmitting personality. The screen may not convey *true* character, and it loses a personality's strength somewhere between the lens and the screen, but at least it shows what a person looks like, his physical characteristics and mannerisms. It gives an immediate impression of someone, even if it's not necessarily the right impression.

The ability of television to bring outside events into the living-room has given it an air of magic which has tended to push radio into the background. It's the accepted stage for making stars out of people — faces known to millions — be they singers, businessmen, politicians or comics.

That's all right if it's only your personality that you want to project. But the intrusion of personality, with all the distractions like background, gestures and cutting from one face to another, makes it that much harder for people to get the *message*.

And that's where radio scores: with the message. As one entertainer put it: 'The trouble with television is that the picture gets in the way.'

The fact is that people actually *listen* to the radio. They certainly listen to it more than television. People often say of a radio programme: 'Turn that off, it's just talk.'

That's actually a compliment to radio. What they mean is that if they left it on they'd feel obliged to listen. Radio's fine as background so long as it's playing music. People happily clean the house, do the ironing, paint the back door or drive along to the soothing sounds of records that all sound the same, but once the talk show starts their mood changes. Within minutes they do one of three things: they turn it off, or switch programmes, *or they start listening.*

Then of course there's a bunch of others who are already listening because they want to. Either way, your own message as the interviewee has a relatively more attentive listener than on television.

So with people listening to the *words,* you're well placed to communicate your *ideas.* On radio the listener is practically sitting there saying: 'Come on, what have you got to tell me?' In contrast, the television viewer is sitting there like an overfed Roman consul saying: 'Amuse me.'

A receptive audience isn't the only advantage of radio. Here are some others:

It's friendlier

Radio journalists slip the old knuckledusters on from time to time, and you'll never be immune from trap-door questions, but in general radio tends to be more concerned with interesting the listener than with crucifying the interviewee.

This doesn't mean you can relax. In fact, if anything it requires even more concentration, as we'll see in the next chapter. But at least you will usually get a fair hearing on radio, and they can't show any sneaky bits of film that you didn't know about!

There's more coverage

In Britain alone there are some 40 local radio stations and in America the number runs into the thousands. This means that radio stations are hungry for news. Some do little else but play pop music, in fact, but the rest are often desperate for material of local interest.

When you have something to publicize it's more than likely that there's a radio station in your area which would love to hear about it. National programmes, too, need plenty of items to fill the air time of the various chat shows and news bulletins, and they reach a much bigger audience. After all, there are 850 million radio sets in the world.

And don't forget all those people driving along in their cars with nothing to do but listen to the radio.

It's cheaper

Radio is infinitely cheaper to run than television, which is good news when it comes to outside interviewing.

On the occasions when you're too busy to get away to the studio, or you would be happier doing it at the office or at home anyway, it's little effort for them to send someone round to record an interview *in situ*. No cameras. No technicians. No lighting. Simply one person and a portable tape-recorder.

Again, this increases the likelihood of getting some welcome publicity when you want it.

It's all too easy to regard radio as the poor relation of television when in fact it's a great medium for communicating ideas and messages to a fairly attentive audience. Continue, of course, to seek television coverage for your product, but remember radio as well. It can double the publicity and will often come over more effectively.

18. Radio interview techniques

The techniques for radio interviews are basically similar to those for television, but there are a few important differences.

Preparation

The decision on whether to do it or not and the information required from the producers is the same (except that: for 'any film or props?', read 'any other material I should know about?'). The preparation must be just as painstaking and thorough and *you must still learn your brief.*

Stick to two or three key points, with three or four subpoints for each. *Anecdotes* are, if anything, even more crucial. A short story, a parable, a brief tale of success or disaster — your radio listener will lap it up.

The same goes for the analogies. The television viewer expects to be shown a picture of something all the time, but the radio listener is used to having to paint his own mental pictures. This is why quite a few successful radio shows ('The Goons', for example) never really make it on television. So you put as much of your material as possible into everyday images for the listener.

One nice difference in the preparation — you don't have to worry about how you look. For all the listener knows, you could be sitting there in the nude!

The studio

Radio studios are generally smaller than their television counterparts, and you usually sit at a table with a microphone right in front of you.

Surprisingly, a radio studio can be more distracting than a TV one. They come in all shapes and sizes, but the biggest difference is that you can see what's going on.

The lights in a *television* studio are so bright that you're lucky if you can see the cameraman, so you sit there in a cocoon and can concentrate on your message. But in a *radio* studio you can see the technicians behind the soundproof glass, and there are dozens of other distractions.

An attractive girl suddenly drifts across your line of vision to hand a note to the interviewer just as you're holding forth on the merits of spectroscopic analysis in the diagnosis of duodenal ulcers in earthworms. Or a face appears behind the glass, mouthing 'We're going to the bar — see you there in five minutes', and it's not unknown in a prolonged programme for the coffee cups to be passed round.

I was involved in one long programme where a panel of experts was discussing the Budget, trying not to clink the teaspoons in the saucers. An eminent businessman was in full swing on the inflationary effects of public spending, when a folded piece of paper was thrust urgently in front of him. Trying to maintain his composure and to keep talking, he carefully unfolded it and glanced at the message. It said quite simply: 'Pass the sugar'!

Voice test

They need to test your voice for the same reason as on television. Remember to speak at the level you intend to use for the rest of the interview. Unlike television, you can't ignore the microphone. In a radio studio it usually emerges from the desk or wall and hovers just in front of your nose. You have to face it and speak into it all the time.

Manner

It's still a good idea to sit forward in your chair even though people can't see you, because it's as important as ever to stay wide awake and in command of things.

And it's even more important to speak clearly and distinctly. At least on television the viewer is able to do a spot of lip-reading to aid comprehension, but the radio listener has only your voice.

Of course, you can relax the rules about mannerisms and

gestures. The listener can't see your good or bad side and can't tell if you're smoking, twitching or suffering from measles.

No thinking time

Don't go mad on note-reading, though. It's tempting to assume that as no one can see you it's less important to learn the brief. But in fact it's more important than ever.

This is because there's *no time to think on radio.* When really cornered on television you can resort to some of the ploys we mentioned — cleaning spectacles, nose-blowing, pipe-lighting, etc. It works because the viewer is watching to see what you do next. But all you get on radio is *silence,* which you can't afford. The interview has to keep flowing, so your answers must follow bang on the end of the questions.

So, on both radio and television there's no substitute for knowing in advance *what* you want to say and *how* you're going to say it. Nevertheless, it's much easier on radio to refer to your notes for guidance. By all means *look* at them, so long as you don't read from them or rustle the paper.

Sincerity, enthusiasm

This is where radio starts to get difficult. In front of a camera there are two ways of demonstrating enthusiasm and sincerity — the way you *look* and the way you *sound.*

But the microphone only picks up the latter, so you have to get everything over with your voice. It's not easy. No matter how often you've said whatever it is you're saying, sound *interested.* Remember that your listener hasn't heard it before, so throw some effort into it. Vary the pitch and speed.

As with television, learn from others. Listen to radio for yourself and try to work out why some succeed and others don't. Some people seem to jump out of the speaker at you. They sound alive and involved with their subjects. You find yourself listening intently for the next gem of information.

Aim to emulate the winners yourself and you won't go far wrong.

Good radio interviewers are as good at their job as any television interviewer, and will keep things moving, giving you only 15 to 20 seconds at a time to say your bit. Only too often, though, you'll come across radio interviewers who simply don't have the knack of keeping an interview alive.

This is especially true on the smaller stations, where you may be interviewed by a rookie who's learning the trade. He asks you a few questions from his note pad and leaves you for a couple of minutes to get on with it.

It plays hell with the impression you give of enthusiasm. Immersed in your subject you start to drone away while the listener's mind turns to what to cook for supper that night. So work on explaining your key points with plenty of life and zeal and say what you have to say in the shortest possible time.

If for some reason the interviewer still hasn't got the message that it's time for another question — perhaps he's dried up or is choking on his coffee (which is a likely occurrence if the BBC's coffee is anything to go by) — then *take yourself* into the next key point. A quick pause for breath, and 'While we're on the subject of aircraft safety, you might be surprised to hear that the airframe of a plane makes as much noise as the engines. That roaring noise you hear as a jumbo flies over your garden while you're out there having a quiet snooze on a Sunday afternoon . . .'

Interview techniques
Otherwise the same rules apply to handling a radio interview as we've discussed in 'Winning the battle'.

It's worth flicking back to that chapter now and running through the lessons learnt from Will E Makit's experience, picturing yourself in a radio studio with a big microphone in front of your face. Look specially hard at the bits about anecdotes and analogies.

Training

Most training courses cater for television, though many incorporate a bit of radio work somewhere in the course. Since the techniques are basically the same you might as well learn it all at once.

But where you really score with radio is in self-training, because all you need for a mock radio studio is a room and a cassette or tape-recorder! You can also practise on your own at sounding lively and enthusiastic.

Programmes

As with television, the radio programmes most likely to involve you fall into the categories of: news (main and diary), documentary (investigative and descriptive), and specialist. The radio shows in which the host or DJ plays records, and in between has guests in the studio for a few minutes at a time, are similar to the TV diary programmes. They are out to interest and inform listeners, not reduce the interviewee to tears.

Types of interview

The interview types are pretty much the same, but some special handling is required for some of them:

Face-to-face

This is what we've been working on, where you and the interviewer(s) do your stuff in the studio.

Panel

Groups of experts, or people who disagree with one another, come over well on radio. The trouble is that it's harder to get attention. There's no director to turn the camera on you when you start jumping up and down, so you have to speak out at the right moment and be that little bit more forceful.

Straight-to-microphone

It's highly unlikely that any radio producer is ever going to say to you: 'We're interested in your annual accounts. Here's a studio, just sit there for two minutes and talk about them.' But you never know.

If for some reason you ever do find yourself sitting all alone in front of the mike then you're on to a good thing. A radio presentation is more credible to the listener because it doesn't have the 'big brother' effect of a face filling the screen, telling you to vote for it.

More than ever, really work at being *interesting*. Any kind of presentation must have at least one story in it to grip the listener's attention. Use analogies instead of jargon. Vary the pitch of your voice and don't rush at it, don't gabble. Use notes by all means, but don't read the material out.

Down-the-line

This is hell. It's bad enough in a TV studio, but at least there you have a camera to look at. In a down-the-line radio interview you just sit there in solitary confinement, totally disembodied from the interviewer and any other participants. There are just two things to remember: your brief and your voice. A well-prepared, thoroughly learnt brief is something you can cling to, something you can refer to for the things you want to say. Then be firm and clear when you speak. It's almost like talking boldly to yourself on a dark night to keep the bogeymen away.

Beyond that there's not much help to offer. It's a lousy way of doing an interview, and you'll just have to do the best you can.

Telephone

The telephone gives radio producers an easy means of interviewing all sorts of people at short notice, at any time of day, and in any location. It's also a popular way of obtaining the view of the general public on 'phone-in' programmes.

Used properly, the telephone can provide you with a good interview. All that's required is some preparation beforehand and the right kind of handling.

For a start, you can set your own stage for a telephone interview. Whether at home or at the office, you can choose how you want to sit and — to some extent — which room you use. You're in your own territory, which is a psychological advantage.

As with any interview outside the studio, make sure there are no interruptions. If in the office, give instructions for incoming calls to go to someone else and get someone to stand guard over the office door. At home, send the kids out, put the dog out of earshot and lock the doors. Wherever you are, don't be too close to a busy road or other noise source.

With a telephone you don't have to worry about echo from an empty room: a telephone is less sophisticated than a microphone and therefore less choosy about the acoustics, but what is *essential* is that you don't try to listen to the interview on the radio at the same time.

If you have the radio on anywhere near the telephone it

transmits its own signal back down the phone, and so back to itself over the air. The signal goes round in circles at ever-increasing speed until it emits an ear-piercing shriek. This whine is called 'feed-back' and is guaranteed to ruin any phone-in. If you want to hear the interview, leave the radio on in another room and record it.

But the really crucial thing with a telephone interview is your *voice*. This is the big disadvantage. Even on a clear line your voice loses a lot of quality and takes on a tinny effect. Add a few of the crackles and distortions that telephone companies put into their lines and you start to sound like you're being interviewed in a tin shack in a hailstorm. All impact is lost.

So the great thing with the telephone is to just about halve your normal speaking rate and be *crisp* and *clear*. Pretend the interviewer has his ear to the phone and there's a plug of cotton wool in that ear. Don't bellow, just lift your voice slightly and enunciate each word so that he can hear it through the cotton wool.

Watch out, too, for the sneaky last word. It's quite easy for a hostile interviewer to finish with a loaded remark, and you argue back only to find you've been talking to yourself. If you've been maligned and have a genuine grievance, phone them right back and insist that the record is put straight.

Outside interviews
The scope for outside radio interviews is almost unlimited. There's no problem with lighting and no expensive equipment. In the last analysis a radio interview can be done by one person with a portable recorder at very little cost. I've seen an important interview for a national radio programme conducted with a cassette recorder on the table after lunch, with the two participants switching off after each question and discussing what to say next over a bottle of wine. The recorder must have been switched off and on 20 times and the whole performance took half an hour, yet the result at the end of the day was a crisp, three-minute piece that sounded like an impromptu performance by a couple of pros.

That's another advantage of a recorder — at virtually no extra cost you can do any number of takes in order to get the best edited result. They'll sometimes do a few takes in a recorded studio interview, too, but it ties up expensive studio time so is less popular.

Radio moguls are sticklers for sound quality though, so they still prefer to get you into the studio where your voice can be pasteurised through millions of pounds' worth of electronic gadgetry. Failing that there are mobile studios and radio cars which can transmit live material, though these are more commonly used for things like sporting events.

Watch out for the fact that an interview on tape or cassette is, of course, recorded. This is generally an advantage, as most radio people will edit in the best interests of a lively broadcast, but if there are likely to be problems it's best to insist on a live studio interview to be certain of fair treatment.

Outdoor and indoor interviews are much of a muchness in the case of radio. Be sure, again, to avoid distractions like overhead aircraft, ringing telephones and hollow, empty rooms.

That is, unless you actually *want* some sound effects. There might be a case for our old friend Will E Makit doing his interview to the background noise of thousands of happily cackling hens. Someone protesting at juggernauts driving through his village could make his point more effectively if interviewed in the high street where his words are obliterated at frequent intervals by the roar of a 20-tonner.

'Doorstepping' is just as popular on radio as on television. 'We're waiting here outside the courtroom to see if we can grab a few words with the Chairman . . .' As ever, it provides you with an opportunity to get a message of your own over: 'The negotiations are still going on, but what I *can* tell you is . . .'

CHECK-LIST

1. Thorough *preparation,* and learning your brief, are just as important for radio as for television.
   - ☐ Stick to 2 or 3 key points.
   - ☐ *Anecdotes* are crucial.
   - ☐ So are *analogies.*

2. The studio is usually small, with a big microphone in front of your nose. There are more distractions than in a TV studio.

3. You can't afford *pauses.* No thinking space.

4. The listener can't see you, so sound sincere and enthusiastic.
   - ☐ If the interviewer fails to get things moving, get them moving yourself.

5. The types of interview are the same as television:
   - ☐ Face-to-face.
   - ☐ Panel. Speak up and speak out when you want to say your piece.
   - ☐ Straight-to-microphone. More convincing than straight-to-camera. Keep it lively.
   - ☐ Down-the-line. Miserable. Use your *brief* and your *voice* as aids.
   - ☐ Telephone. Convenient, on your territory, but poor sound quality. Avoid feed-back from radio in same room. Speak clearly.
   - ☐ Outside. Recorded interviews cheap and easy — can do lots of takes. Avoid distracting noises, except as deliberate sound effects.

19. Local radio

British radio and television may be streets ahead of their American counterparts in the responsibility and quality of programmes, but the Americans can't be touched for size, and they have every right to laugh at Britain's 'new' development in establishing local radio stations.

For the average American the local radio station is as much a part of life as the local bank. The total number of radio stations in the US is a mind-blowing 8400 — that's one for every 25,000 people. If you can bear with a few more figures: 98 out of every 100 Americans have a radio in the home and 93 out of 100 cars in America are equipped with one.

Radio is by far the major source of news for most people. A recent Opinion Research Corporation poll showed that radio is the primary news source for 57 per cent of US adults, compared with only 19 per cent for television and 18 per cent for newspapers.

As with television, the news content of programmes is on the increase and with talk shows and phone-ins becoming ever more popular, local radio can be a valuable PR asset for the businessman.

Local radio has long been a fact of life in America, but in Britain it's relatively new. Like the internal combustion engine it used to be something that 'just wouldn't catch on', but in recent years the growth has been spectacular.

There are now some 40 local stations in the UK, both BBC and independent, and a further 60 groups waiting in the wings, anxious to establish stations. It's a logical development. After all, there are nearly 1000 newspapers, each requiring more staff than a small radio station. People like to hear local news and information and advertisers will pay for air time in the region where their customers are.

Programme content varies from station to station. Some, like the 'pirate' stations, put out nothing but deafening music round the clock, while at the other end of the scale you have programmes like LBC specializing in news and current affairs.

Wherever you live it's likely that there's a radio station somewhere in your area, and that there's room for you to promote your case for free.

Local stations are generally run on a shoestring, so with a limited reporting staff they're delighted to have people come to them with material. And whatever your company or pressure group, there's bound to be a story in it from time to time. Are you expanding? Cutting down? Fighting the Council over something? Do you have a new product? Are you organizing a charity function? Making a profit? A loss? Local radio will take material which a national station wouldn't look at — so long as it's of local interest.

Having decided on your story, let them judge for themselves. Simply phone your local station and ask for the news editor. Explain who you are and what you have to say. Maybe that particular story isn't what they want, so make sure they've got your number and can call you whenever something in your line comes up.

Local radio coverage has several advantages for you. For one thing, it's almost always favourable — you'll get a fair chance for some good propaganda. It's also a great opportunity to have regular practice. You may only get on national radio or TV once every few months, but it's quite possible to have frequent local radio slots.

Of course, you can buy local radio advertising time quite cheaply, but the pros and cons of that are best left to the admen. Besides, why pay for something you can get free, and with much more credibility?

Take the case history of the British Insurance Association. They started their free advertising campaign by taking a professional trainer round their branches to groom local spokesmen. Meanwhile a press officer would put the spokesman in touch with the nearest radio station with the message: 'This is Mr X. Any time there's an insurance question he's the guy to talk to.'

Once the radio stations realized they had a ready source of information, with an articulate spokesman thrown in for good measure, they started to create a regular requirement for such information. When a building burned down they'd get on to the local BIA man to ask about the insurance implications. When house prices rocketed they'd invite the insurance expert along to advise listeners to increase their premiums.

In the first full year of the campaign the BIA had 150 radio slots and it has reached a stage now where some local stations even have a weekly 'Insurance phone-in'. Mr BIA sits in the studio and answers listeners' questions with infinitely more credibility than a straight ad.

Over the years the Association has achieved air time worth millions at minimal initial cost.

Epilogue

I have a friend who lives in a small Norfolk town. Though getting on in years he is one of those remarkable men who won't ease up. He races yachts, runs a shop, shoots targets and game with unnerving accuracy, maintains a wildfowl reserve, is a leading expert on weapons and flies out in helicopters to remote islands as an official seal-culler.

On top of that he's a great raconteur, so it was inevitable that someone should do a television programme about him. For weeks a film crew followed him everywhere, from his living room to the middle of the North Sea. Then someone tipped them off that one of his skills was the rare ability to shoot two pheasants in flight, one after the other, with a double-barrelled shotgun.

This just had to be filmed, but unfortunately it was high summer and pheasant shooting isn't allowed till autumn. So they held the programme and came back in the autumn to film the pheasant episode.

Dawn was the best time for it, he told them. At dawn they set off — marksman and dog, producer and cameraman creeping stealthily through the undergrowth till they reached a quarry. The dog suddenly sniffed game, rushed off and put up two pheasants.

From years of experience my friend acted instinctively. Safety catch off, gun into the shoulder, the barrels swung through the birds' line of flight.

'I knew it would make a great picture', he said. 'They were flying across the low, red, rising sun and the cameraman was just behind my right shoulder. My gun arced with them till they were smack in the centre of that big red ball, then I squeezed the trigger twice inside one second. Two shots close together and both birds dropped in mid-flight.'

135

Satisfied, he lowered his smoking gun barrel and asked the producer: 'That what you wanted?'

'It was perfect,' she said, 'but I'm afraid the camera missed the first pheasant. Would you mind doing it again please?'

That true story epitomizes the gulf of misunderstanding between the people inside television and those outside it. Television is nothing more than a lot of people making programmes about a lot of other people, yet each side fails to understand what makes the others tick.

Considering that television is one of the biggest things ever to happen to human communications — and it's been around for 40 years or more — the levels of ignorance are incredible.

This is especially true where business is concerned, and if nothing else, this book may have helped to break down one or two barriers.

I've already been criticized by both businessmen and television producers about the contents. When both sides of an argument criticize you it's a good sign. The same businessmen who pour out press releases daily to the newspapers still run for cover when invited to put their case on television. And television people hate the idea of businessmen arming themselves for a fight before entering the studios.

No apologies to either side, I'm afraid. Television is an alien world and no newcomer should enter it without the basic survival kit of the early chapters. But at the same time it offers untold benefits for communicating important messages and getting through to Joe Public as never before, and only very occasionally are there any real reasons for avoiding the cameras.

So go in there with both barrels and hit your pheasants — and when you do hit them, just hope that the cameras are rolling!